YOUR BODY

INCREDIBLE BUT TRUE FACTS

This edition published by Parragon Books Ltd in 2016
and distributed by

Parragon Inc.
440 Park Avenue South, 13th Floor
New York, NY 10016
www.parragon.com

Consultants: Dr. Sue Mann and Dr. Clare J. Ray

ISBN 978-1-4748-5034-6

Printed in China

YOUR BODY

INCREDIBLE BUT TRUE FACTS

PaRragon

Bath • New York • Cologne • Melbourne • Delhi
Hong Kong • Shenzhen • Singapore

CONTENTS

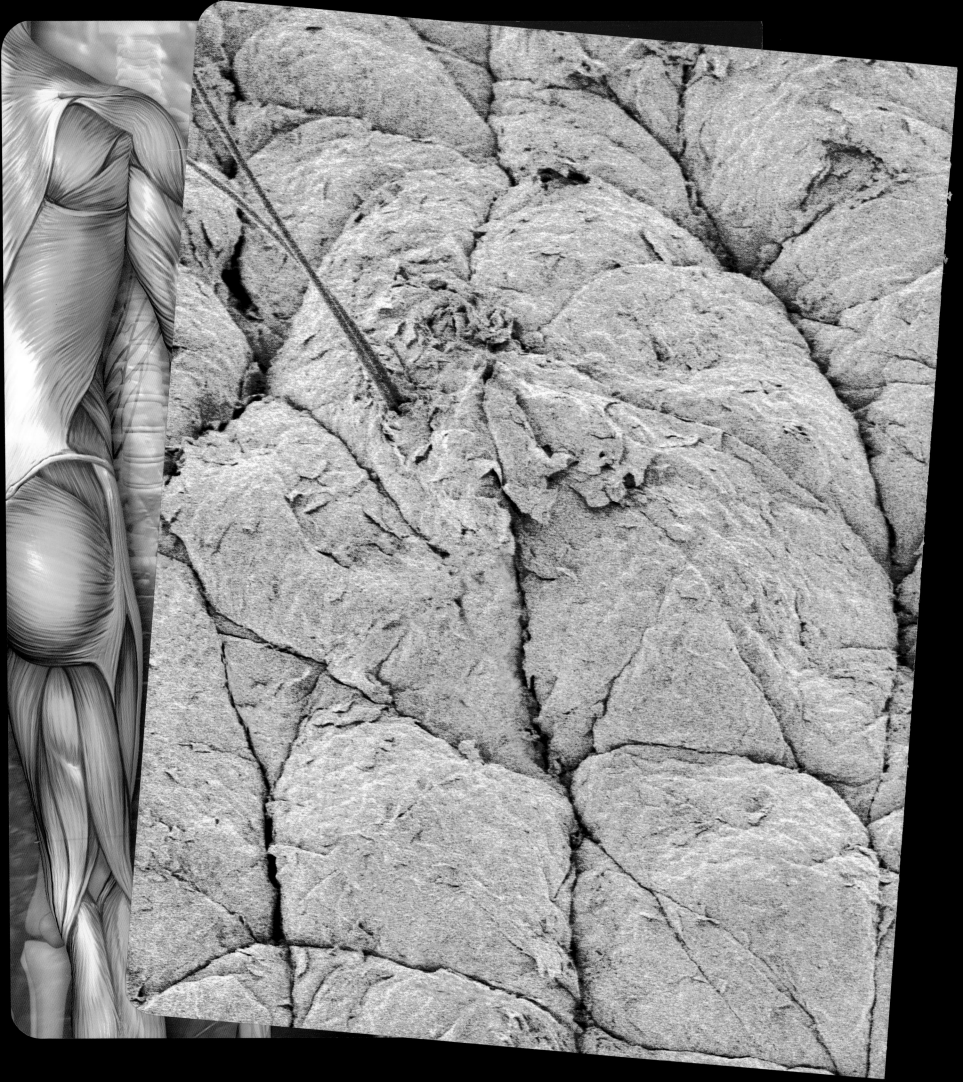

SKIN, HAIR, AND NAILS

When we look at other people, what we see is not alive—except for their eyes! The body's outermost layer is made of tiny dead flakes of skin. Hair and nails, too, are no longer living. However, just beneath the surface, your skin is alive and busy. It covers our entire bodies, protects us from bumps, helps to control our body temperature, and gives us our sense of touch.

A Closer Look at Skin

Your skin forms a tough barrier to keep out dirt, germs, and harmful rays from the sun. It also stops your body from losing important fluids, salts, and other substances. The skin, hair, and nails together are known as the body's integumentary, or covering, system.

Skin's Outer Layer

Look through a microscope and you will see that skin has two layers. The outermost or upper layer is called the epidermis. This is made up mostly of dead skin cells and it provides the body's main protection. The epidermis varies in thickness on different parts of the body. Where there is more wear, such as on the soles of the feet, friction and rubbing cause the epidermis to grow thicker.

Fingerprints

The tips of your fingers have ridges of skin forming patterns of swirls, curls, and loops, known as fingerprints. They help the skin to grip well. Every person has a unique pattern of fingerprints. A few animals, such as koalas, have fingerprints, too.

The Inner Layer

Beneath the epidermis is the lower layer of skin, which is called the dermis. The dermis is very flexible because it has tiny strands or fibers that allow it to stretch easily and then spring back into shape. The dermis also holds the roots of your skin's hairs (see right).

It's Amazing!

Every year, about 4.5 pounds of your skin is rubbed off and flakes away. That's enough to fill a bucket!

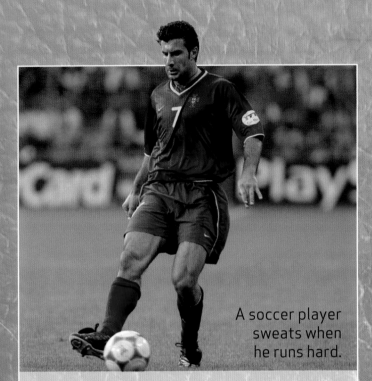

A soccer player sweats when he runs hard.

Top Facts

- The total skin area of an average adult body would, if laid out flat, cover nearly 22 square feet.

- The weight of an adult's skin is around 6.5 pounds.

- The skin on the eyelids is only two-hundredths of an inch thick.

- The skin on the soles of the feet can be about a quarter-inch thick.

Cooling Sweat

When your body gets hot, your skin releases sweat. This is called perspiration. The sweat flows out onto the skin's surface and draws heat from the body as it evaporates (turns into vapor). Even when cool, your body still makes small amounts of sweat, which is known as insensible perspiration.

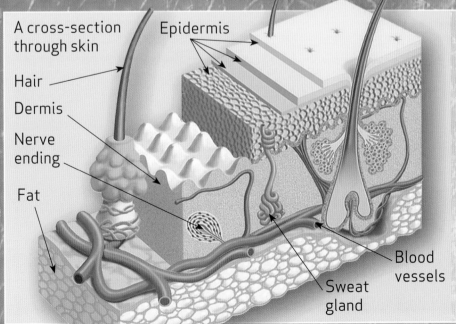

A cross-section through skin

Epidermis

Hair

Dermis

Nerve ending

Fat

Sweat gland

Blood vessels

Under the Surface

The dermis layer of the skin is packed with millions of microscopic parts such as blood vessels, nerve endings for touch, pain and temperature, and glands that make sweat. Just under the dermis is a layer of soft fat, which acts like a cushion to absorb bumps.

Always Growing

Your skin may look the same from one day to the next, but tiny flakes are falling off or being rubbed away all the time. This does not, however, leave you red and sore, because there are always more flakes forming to replace the lost ones.

A Busy Place

The epidermis constantly renews itself. Like all body parts, it is made of millions of microscopic "building blocks" called cells. At the base of the epidermis these cells are very active. They continually split in two, to make more cells. These new cells gradually move toward the surface. They are pushed upward as more and more new cells form beneath them.

A microscopic view of skin cells flaking off

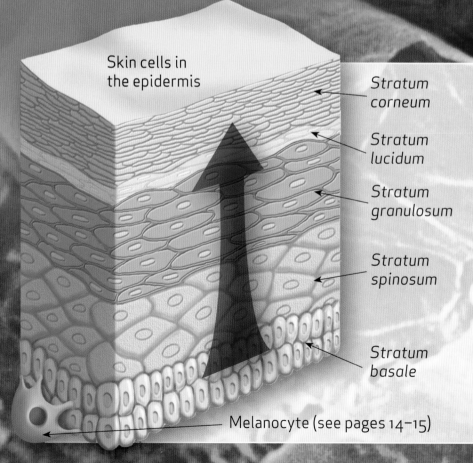

Skin cells in the epidermis

Stratum corneum

Stratum lucidum

Stratum granulosum

Stratum spinosum

Stratum basale

Melanocyte (see pages 14–15)

Epidermal Layers

Cells multiply at the base of the epidermis, becoming flatter as they are pushed upward. As they flatten, the cells die and become very hard. This flattening also produces a series of layers in the epidermis. From the bottom, these layers are the *stratum basale*, the *stratum spinosum*, the *stratum granulosum*, the *stratum lucidum*, and the *stratum corneum*.

It's Amazing!

Up to one million dead skin cells fall off your skin every single minute. When you rub yourself dry after a shower or bath, even more wear away!

Chemicals and Skin

The skin does not protect us completely. Some chemicals, such as pesticides, can seep through skin into the tissues and blood, and spread around the body, causing harmful effects. Protective clothing, goggles, and gloves help to keep these chemicals off the skin.

Wearing protective gloves is very important when handling chemicals.

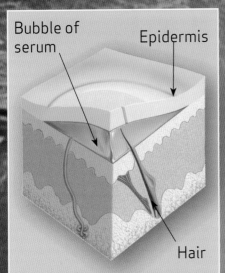

Bubble of serum

Epidermis

Hair

Cross-section of a blister

Up, Up, and Away

As the epidermal cells move up, they change. They begin as box shapes and then slowly become flatter, like paving stones. They also become filled with a substance called keratin, which makes the skin cells tough and hard. Eventually, the cells become so full of keratin that they die. But they are still pushed upward by more new cells below. After a journey lasting about four weeks, the flattened cells reach the surface. Here, they finally wear away as you move around, rub inside your clothes, and press against things.

Friction Blisters

A friction blister happens when the epidermis suffers sudden rubbing and wear. The top layers of the skin separate from the tissue beneath. Clear fluid, called serum, leaks from blood vessels and collects to form a "bubble" under the outer layer.

Rubbing Your Skin

- Spread out a clean, flat, black plastic sheet, such as a trash bag.
- Carefully rub your forearms or legs over the sheet. Not too hard—do not scratch or leave red marks.
- Look closely at the sheet. Can you see tiny pale specks? That's your skin. At least, it used to be!

Skin Color

People's skin color varies, even within the same family. The basic color of our skin is inherited from our parents, but it gets darker if we go out in the sun frequently. This is most noticeable in people who have pale skin to start with.

Melanin

Skin color comes from tiny particles of pigment, a type of dark substance, called melanin. These particles are made by cells called melanocytes, which lie at the base of the epidermis. The melanocytes give their melanin to the surrounding skin cells. Strong sunlight makes the skin produce more melanin and go darker, which is known as a suntan.

Make sure your skin is protected by regularly applying sunscreen.

Sunscreen

Protecting the skin against strong sunlight is very important, because it reduces the risk of skin cancer. Sunscreen lotions and creams filter out the harmful rays, especially UVB (ultraviolet B). Such rays can pass through thin clouds, so you should wear sunscreen protection even on hazy summer days.

It's Amazing!

There are more than 10,000 melanocytes in an area of skin about the size of a fingernail. This number is basically the same for everybody. In people with darker skin, the melanocytes are more active and make more melanin.

No Color

Very rarely, the skin produces little or no coloring substances. The result is an overall white or pale pink coloration of skin, hair, and eyes, known as albinism. This can happen in animals, such as this peacock (right), and in humans, too.

An albino peacock

Sunburn

The higher amounts of melanin in suntanned skin help to protect the skin and body parts beneath from the sun's rays. If strong sunlight shines on pale skin, it can cause painful sunburn, with redness and blisters forming in just an hour or two.

A group of children with different skin colors

Pigment Cells

Melanocytes have long, fingerlike extensions, called dendrites. These dendrites produce tiny particles of melanin. The melanin passes into surrounding cells, which then begin their journey to the surface (see page 12).

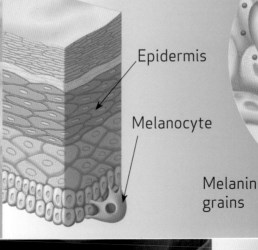

Epidermis

Melanocyte

Melanin grains

Melanocyte dendrites

Temperature Control

Humans, like cats, dogs, and other mammals, are warm-blooded. To work well and stay healthy, the human body needs to stay at a regular, warm temperature of about 98.6 degrees Fahrenheit. The skin plays a vital role in keeping this temperature steady.

Skin hairs stand on end to keep warm air next to the body.

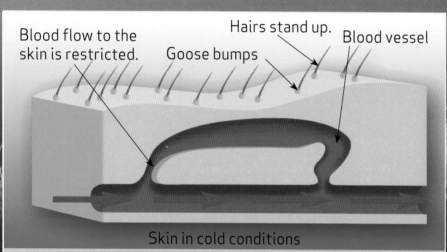

Blood flow to the skin is restricted.

Hairs stand up.

Goose bumps

Blood vessel

Skin in cold conditions

Saving Heat

If the body becomes cold, the small blood vessels that lie near to the surface of the skin get narrower. This is called vasoconstriction. Less blood goes from the inside of the body to carry heat to the skin. This reduces loss of body warmth. Because less blood flows near the skin, it can make you look pale.

Getting Too Cold

In cold weather, miniature muscles pull the skin's tiny hairs upright, forming "goose bumps." The upright hairs trap a layer of air next to the skin, which helps to keep in body warmth. Your body's large muscles make small, fast movements to produce extra heat. This is called shivering.

It's Amazing!

The body has more than two million sweat glands. In very hot conditions they can produce almost 2 quarts of sweat every hour. The water lost in sweat must be replaced by drinking a lot to avoid dehydration.

Keeping Warm

At the end of strenuous exercise, such as running a marathon, the body is hot due to muscle activity. In cold conditions, a hot body can cool down too quickly. Shiny metal foil reflects heat and keeps in body warmth. It stops long-distance runners from getting too cold.

Runners wrapped in metallic blankets at the end of the New York City Marathon

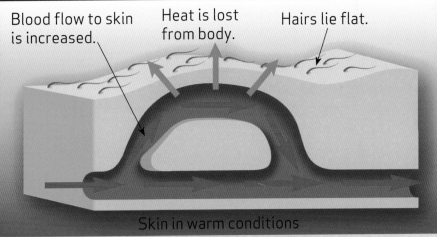

Blood flow to skin is increased.

Heat is lost from body.

Hairs lie flat.

Skin in warm conditions

Top Facts

- If the body gets seriously hot, above 104°F, this is called hyperthermia or heatstroke.

- The body must be slowly cooled back to normal and rehydrated with plenty of drinks.

- If the body gets dangerously cold, below 95°F, this is called hypothermia or exposure.

- The body must be warmed gradually, preferably under medical supervision.

Losing Heat

When the body is hot, small blood vessels near the skin's surface widen. This is known as vasodilation. Vasodilation increases blood flow to the skin, which brings more heat from the body's interior. This increases the amount of heat that is lost to the air. As more blood flows to the skin, it can make you look flushed.

Getting Too Hot

In hot weather and when you exercise, your body heats up. Sweat glands produce watery sweat to help cool the body (see page 11). The tiny hairs on your skin also lie flat so that they do not stop air from flowing over your skin and taking away excess heat.

Cuts and Wounds

The skin is your body's first defense against bumps and hits. Small cuts, scratches, and bruises are common and the skin can repair these small wounds by itself. Bigger injuries may need help, such as stitches to close the wound and a bandage to cover it.

Sealing the Wound

As soon as skin is injured, blood leaks from its tiny vessels. The vessels narrow to reduce the amount of blood loss. The damage also causes cell fragments, or platelets (see pages 92–93), to stick together. Then, substances in the blood form microscopic strands or fibers, called fibrin. The fibers and platelets build up and trap red blood cells, forming a sticky lump called a clot. The clot stops more blood from leaking out and prevents dirt and germs from getting in.

An ice hockey player with a black (bruised) eye

Bruises

A bruise is blood that leaks from damaged blood vessels under the skin. It can be red, blue, or purple at first, but then changes to yellow as the blood slowly breaks down.

How Skin Heals

As a blood clot starts to form, white blood cells leak out of nearby blood vessels and enter the wound to deal with any possible infection (see pages 96–97). Once a hard scab has formed, dividing skin cells in the epidermis form a new layer of skin.

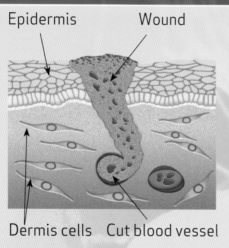

Epidermis   Wound

Dermis cells   Cut blood vessel

1. Damage caused to blood vessel

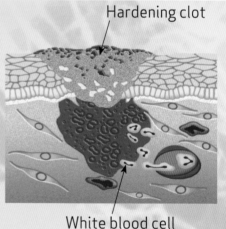

Hardening clot

White blood cell

2. Blood clot starts to harden

As Good as New

Gradually, the clot hardens and dries into a tough covering known as a scab. Underneath, the skin's damaged edges begin to grow together, slowly forming new skin and closing the cut. Finally, the dry scab falls off, and the repair is complete. A big cut or wound may leave an area of skin that is slightly thicker and a different color. This is called a scar.

Strands of fibrin (shown in yellow) trap red blood cells and platelets to form a clot.

Top Facts

- Some people are born lacking a substance in the blood that helps the blood to clot after an injury. If they cut themselves, the blood doesn't clot and keeps flowing. This condition is called hemophilia.

- In 1965, scientists discovered which clotting substances were missing. Today, hemophilia can be treated with injections of the missing substances.

It's Amazing!

When skin is repairing a big cut, it produces a million extra microscopic cells every hour to heal the wound.

New skin layer   Scab

Scar tissue

White blood cell

Repaired blood vessel

3. New skin layer forms

4. Scar tissue forms

Hairy Human

Who is hairier—a human being or a gorilla? Actually, they both have a similar number of hairs on their bodies. A human's body hairs are much shorter and thinner in most places, so we notice them less.

Scalp and Body Hair

The human body has different types of hairs on different parts. The main hairs are head or scalp hairs. These are thick and can grow very long if you do not cut them. There are also about five million tiny hairs over most of the body. These body hairs are usually small and soft, especially in babies and children. Only a few areas lack hair completely, such as the palms, the fingers, and the soles of the feet.

It's Amazing!

The number of head hairs varies from one person to the next. People with light or fair hair have about 130,000 hairs. People with brown hair have about 110,000 hairs. People with black hair have about 100,000 hairs, and people with red or ginger hair have about 90,000 hairs.

A balding father and his long-haired daughter

Losing Hair

There are different forms and causes of hair loss and baldness. In typical male-pattern hair loss, hair starts to thin on top of the head as the man gets older. The hairline at the front also recedes and joins the bald patch on top. This process is linked to the male hormone testosterone.

More Types of Hair

Your face has eyebrow and eyelash hairs. Eyebrows help to push aside sweat or rainwater, so it does not drip into the eyes. Eyelashes sweep away tiny bits of floating dust as we blink, so they do not go into the eyes. Adult men and women also have underarm hair, and pubic hair between their legs.

An old man with a beard

Facial Hair

Adult men usually have about 15,000 facial hairs, which can grow to form mustaches and beards. These hairs grow about 5 inches every year.

A male gorilla

How Hairy is a Gorilla?

Great apes, such as gorillas, have longer, coarser body hair than humans, but they also have hair-free areas on their palms, fingers, and soles, like we do. Gorillas have hairless areas on the face and chest, while these parts are much hairier in human males.

Brushing Hair

- Using a new or completely clean hairbrush, brush your hair normally.
- How many hairs come out onto the brush?
- Do this several times through the day, and count the total number of hairs.
- Don't worry—in most people 50 to 100 hairs fall out naturally every day.

How Hair Grows

Hairs can look shiny and smooth or rough and crimped, but they can never "glow with life"—because they are dead! The only living part of a hair is its base, from where it grows and gets longer.

In the Pits

A hair grows from a hair follicle. The hair lengthens as new microscopic cells add to its base or root. The cells quickly become hard and flat, like epidermis cells. The hair cells stick together to form a scaly-looking rod that slowly pushes upward out of the follicle.

It's Amazing!

In most people, if the head hairs are not cut, they will grow to about 5 feet long before falling out naturally.
But some people have unusual hair that can grow longer than 20 feet!

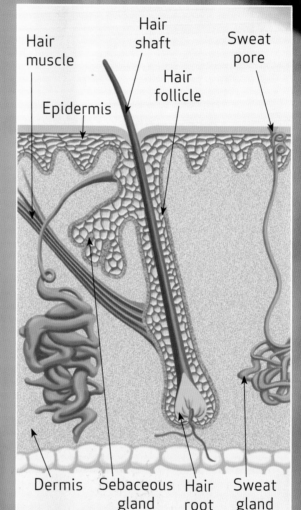

Hair muscle
Hair shaft
Sweat pore
Epidermis
Hair follicle
Dermis
Sebaceous gland
Hair root
Sweat gland

Hair Follicle

The hair follicle is a fold in the epidermis that leads down into the dermis. The hair shaft grows up the follicle to the surface. The hair is linked to a muscle that can pull the follicle so that the hair stands up (see page 16).

Hair Shaft

Under a microscope, you can see the edges of the stuck-together flat cells on a hair shaft. Hair thickness varies from just a thousandth of an inch to more than four times that diameter.

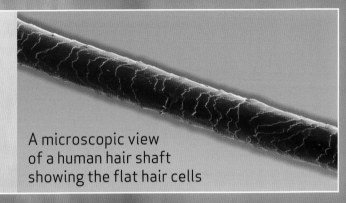

A microscopic view of a human hair shaft showing the flat hair cells

Skin's Natural Oil

Next to each hair follicle is a tiny lump-like part called a sebaceous gland. This makes a slightly greasy substance, called sebum, which is skin's natural oil. It oozes up to the skin's surface and spreads out. Sebum keeps skin soft and supple. It also helps to repel water, and helps to kill germs.

A man with hair styled by cutting it and using chemicals to make it stand on end

Natural Hair

Hair can be straight, wavy, curly, or frizzy. The natural style of your hair depends upon the cross-section of the thousands of hairs on your head, which can be almost circular or nearly flat.

A variety of natural hairstyles

Top Facts

- Head hairs grow by about an eighth of an inch each week.

- Fine, fair hair grows more slowly than thick, dark hair.

- After a hair falls out, the follicle "rests" for up to six months, then a new hair starts to grow from the same follicle.

Fingernails and Toenails

Nails are very useful, and not just for a quick scratch. They help to make the backs of the fingertips stiff, rather than floppy. This lets you judge the pressure of your grip more precisely, so you can pick up a delicate flower or a tiny pin.

How Nails Grow

Like hairs and the outer layer of skin, nails are made of keratin (see page 13). The main sheet, or plate, of the nail is dead. It is only alive at its root, which is hidden under the skin of the finger or toe. As the nail lengthens from its root, it slides along the nail bed, toward the tip of the finger or toe.

It's Amazing!

Most people keep their nails neatly trimmed, to prevent snags and breaks. But some people let them grow and grow, until they reach more than 28 inches long!

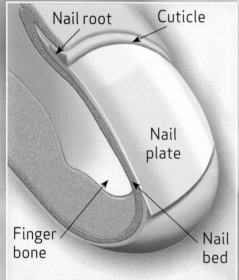

Nail root   Cuticle

Nail plate

Finger bone

Nail bed

Nail Structure

The nail plate is a curved slab of keratin, which sits on the nail bed. Along its bottom edge is the sensitive skin of the nail lateral border, often called the cuticle or "quick."

The tip of the nail that overhangs the nail bed is called the free edge.

Faster and Slower

Most nails grow about a half an inch each month. Fingernails grow slightly faster than toenails, and all nails grow faster in warm weather than in cold conditions. A hit to the nail base can cause damage to the part of the nail forming there. This can create a ridge or lump, which grows along with the rest of the nail until it can be cut away.

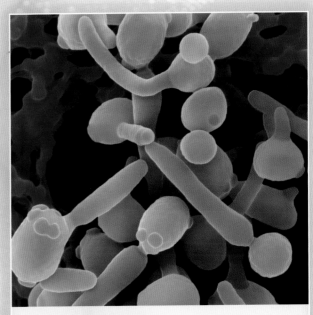

Nail Fungus

Candida albicans (above) is a type of fungus that is fairly common on the human body. Sometimes, however, this fungus can grow out of control and cause infections. This can lead to painful inflammation around the nails, while the nails themselves can become ridged and brittle and change color to green or yellow.

A lion's claws are usually pulled inside its paws so that they stay sharp.

Paws and Claws

Keratin is also the substance that forms animal claws. Unlike your fingernails, a lion's claws are sharpened to a point so that they can tear through and grip any prey.

Nails and Grip

- Before you trim your nails, carefully try to pick up a pin. It should be easy.
- Trim your nails neatly and wash your hands thoroughly.
- Try to pick up the pin again. Short nails, and dry skin without slightly sticky sebum oil, make it much harder.

Skin Marks

Some people have natural marks or patches on their skin. These are normally harmless, but if a skin mark changes in some way, it's best to get expert medical advice.

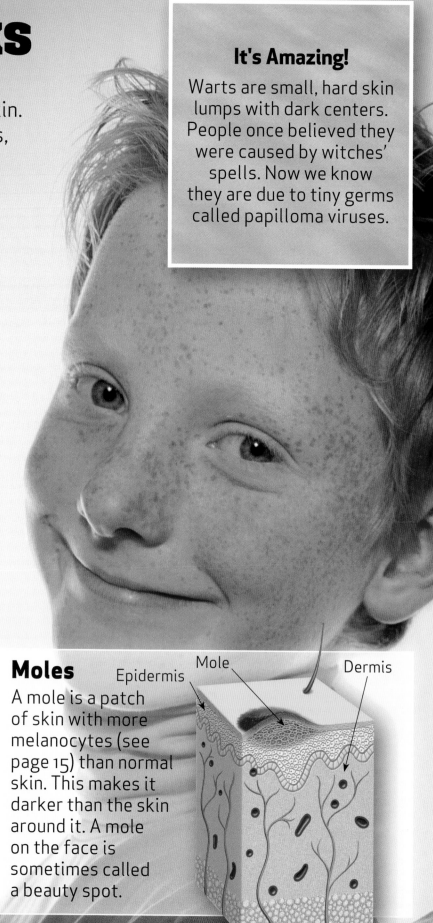

It's Amazing!

Warts are small, hard skin lumps with dark centers. People once believed they were caused by witches' spells. Now we know they are due to tiny germs called papilloma viruses.

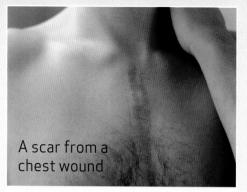

A scar from a chest wound

Scars

After surgery or an accident, the skin might not be able to heal itself fully. This can leave behind scar tissue (see page 19).

Naturally Patchy

Moles are small, dark patches of skin. They usually start to appear at about the age of five or six. Moles that appear late in life or change their appearance (see page 29) should be checked by a doctor. An average person has between 10 and 40 moles of various sizes.

Moles

A mole is a patch of skin with more melanocytes (see page 15) than normal skin. This makes it darker than the skin around it. A mole on the face is sometimes called a beauty spot.

Epidermis   Mole   Dermis

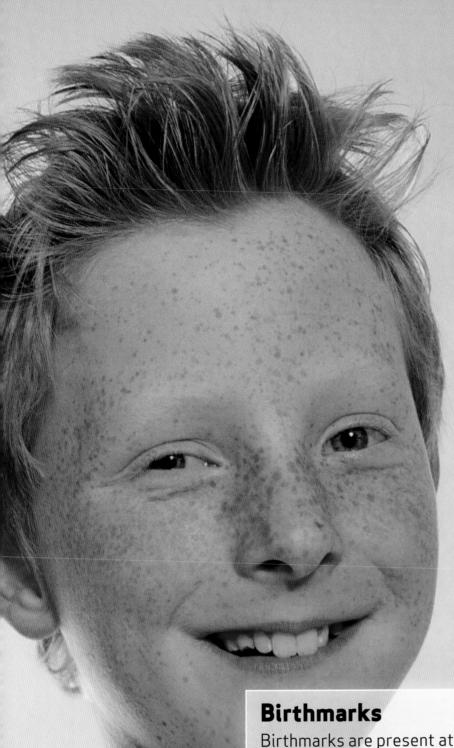

Top Facts

- The Italian and Arabic words for birthmark mean "wish."

- This is because it was believed that they were caused by the mother not fulfilling a sudden wish during her pregnancy.

Freckles

Freckles are small patches of skin that contain more of the natural pigment melanin (see page 14) than the surrounding areas. Freckles tend to occur on the face, shoulders, and arms of people with light skin and fair, reddish, or brown hair. They become more obvious when the skin is exposed to sunlight.

These fair-skinned twins have a lot of freckles on their faces.

Birthmarks

Birthmarks are present at birth, or develop shortly after. Scientists are unsure what causes them, but there are many kinds, such as dark skin patches or strawberry birthmarks, which are lumpy, red patches.

A baby with a birthmark above her lip

Skin Problems

Germs are always floating in the air and landing on our skin. If they get in through a cut or wound, they may cause an infection. Some skin infections—like boils—affect only a small area, while others cause larger marks and rashes on many body parts.

Pimples and Acne

Small pimples called blackheads and whiteheads form when a skin pore or hair follicle gets blocked. The sebum (skin oil) made in the follicle cannot get out, so it builds up and may turn black. When you have more pimples than usual, it is called acne. If germs get into a hair follicle, it swells and becomes a red and painful pimple or boil.

It's Amazing!

Even on healthy skin, there may be more than 1,000 bacteria in an area the size of a fingernail. No wonder we are always being told to wash ourselves regularly.

Historical Cures?

Long ago, people had many strange treatments for skin problems.

- Smear the skin with droppings (dung) from animals, such as cows or sheep.

- Put leeches (worm-like creatures) onto the skin to suck out blood and the "poisons" in it.

- Tie a lump of fresh meat over the mark for a few days and then bury the meat in the earth.

Blocked Pores

Pimples are formed when oily sebum builds up and clogs skin pores. Acne is a skin condition that causes facial pimples and is common during the teenage years. This is due to a change in the natural body hormones in puberty. These hormones make the sebaceous glands more active.

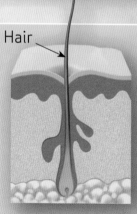

Hair

1. Each hair follicle is an opening for sebum.

Blocked pore

2. The follicle opening, or pore, is blocked with dirt.

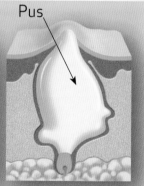

Pus

3. Sebum mixes with pus to form a yellow spot.

Eczema

Eczema is a skin condition where red, itchy patches form. These patches may be dry and scaly, or moist and weeping. The cause of eczema is not clear, but it is often linked with skin that is sensitive or allergic to certain substances, such as soaps, detergents, or cleaners. Some children with eczema have other allergic conditions, such as asthma or hay fever. Many children grow out of these conditions.

A small patch of eczema on a hand. Eczema can spread to cover large parts of the body.

Moles: Changes to Look For

A mole should be shown to a doctor if it changes in some way. The chart below lists some of the changes to look out for, which may mean the mole is harmful.

Normal mole

Normal moles may be concentrated in large numbers on the back, arms, and chest.

Harmful moles

When one half of the mole does not match the other (not symmetrical).

When the edges of the mole are jagged and irregular.

When the color of the mole varies.

When the diameter of the mole is larger than the width of a pencil.

Tattoos

A tattoo is a pattern of colored inks put into the deeper levels of skin, usually by jabbing with some kind of needle. The inks are deep enough to remain for many years and do not grow out as the epidermal skin layer renews itself.

An automatic needle pushing ink under the skin's surface

Skin, Nail, and Hair Care

Our skin has a rough, tough time. Bits of dirt, dust, germs, sweat, and sebum (skin oil) smear onto it every minute of every day. If we don't clean our skin regularly, it becomes dirty and smelly and is at risk of infection and disease.

Good and Bad

Skin is home to a lot of tiny organisms, including bacteria. Some, such as *Proprionibacterium acnes*, are "good." They stop the growth of "bad" bacteria. However, they can turn bad if they reach parts of the body where they shouldn't be, such as deep in a wound.

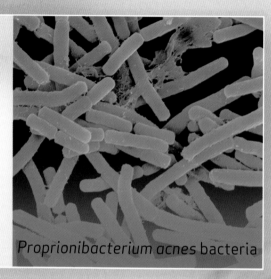

Proprionibacterium acnes bacteria

Keep it Clean

We should wash our hands regularly, especially after going to the bathroom and before we eat or handle food, so we do not transfer germs to the food. Regular washing not only keeps skin clean and healthy and lessens the risks of pimples and rashes; it also helps to prevent other problems, such as food poisoning.

It's Amazing!

If your skin kept growing as usual, but did not wear away at all, it would be as thick as an elephant's skin after just three years!

Staying Trimmed

Whether head hair is short or long, it needs to be washed and brushed regularly, and trimmed occasionally. Medicated shampoos help to reduce tiny pale flakes on the scalp, called dandruff. The more hair is colored, dyed, and heated, the weaker it becomes. Nails are less likely to snag, break, or collect dirt underneath if they are trimmed short.

Washing hands helps to stop the spread of diseases.

Daily Brushing

Brushing or combing hair gets rid of tangles, dust, dirt, and pests. Tangles and knots should be eased out from the hair ends, working toward the roots. Tugging hard at tangles makes them tighter and may damage the hairs or pull them out by their roots.

A microscopic view of a flea

Body Guests

Your skin and hairs may also be home to tiny pests. These include various kinds of fleas, lice, flies, mites, and ticks. The bites from these bugs can cause itchy spots and marks.

The Best Way to Wash?

- After a day outside, using your hands a lot, you need to thoroughly clean your hands.
- First, try rinsing them with just water. How much dirt comes off?
- Next, try using soap and water together. How much dirt comes off?
- Soap removes more dirt than just water, because it sticks to dirt particles and pulls them away from your skin when it is rinsed away.

BONES, JOINTS, AND MUSCLES

Many parts of the body—such as the nerves, gut, and blood vessels—are soft and floppy. But the whole body can stand up straight and strong because it has an inner, supporting framework of bones. Most bones are linked at movable joints and are pulled by powerful muscles. Using bones, joints, and muscles, we can make a wide range of movements, from writing our names to lifting heavy weights, and from leaping in the air to standing on tiptoe.

The Skeleton

All the bones together are called the skeletal system, or skeleton. Each bone is a certain size and shape, depending on its job. The arm and leg bones are long and tube-shaped. The shoulder and hip bones are wide and flat to hold and anchor muscles (see pages 44–45).

Guarding the Body

Some bones are protective. The dome of the skull bone at the top of the head protects the brain. The ribs in the chest are like the bars of a cage, guarding the soft lungs and the pumping heart. The bowl-like shape of the hip bone protects the soft organs of the lower body.

Top Facts

- The human skeleton has a total of 206 bones.
- There are 29 bones in the head and face, 26 in the back, and 25 in the chest.
- There are 64 bones in the shoulders, arms, hands, and fingers and 62 bones in the hips, legs, feet, and toes.

These people are using their bones and muscles to push a car.

Ready, Steady, Push

As we push, muscles hold the skeleton and keep it in a strong position, allowing the bones to take the strain. The legs, back, and arms transfer a forward force to the object being pushed.

Upper skull (cranium)

Lower jaw (mandible)

Neck bones (cervical vertebrae)

Collarbone (clavicle)

Shoulder blade (scapula)

Breastbone (sternum)

Ribs

Forearm bones (ulna, radius)

Finger bones (phalanges)

Upper arm bone (humerus)

Hip bone (pelvis)

Hand bones (carpals)

Lower backbones (lumbar vertebrae)

Not Too Stiff

Bones are hard, but they are not completely rigid, or stiff, especially in children and young people. This means they can bend slightly to take a lot of stress rather than cracking or snapping. Bones are light yet tough—weight for weight, they are stronger than most metals and high-tech plastics. And bones can do what metals and plastics cannot; if they are damaged, they can repair themselves.

The main bones of the human skeleton with their scientific names

Thigh bone (femur)

Kneecap (patella)

Lower leg bones (fibula, tibia)

Foot bones (tarsals)

Toe bones (phalanges)

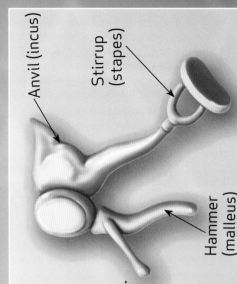

Anvil (incus)

Stirrup (stapes)

Hammer (malleus)

Smallest Bones

The smallest bones are the hammer, anvil, and stirrup inside the ear. Each of these tiny bones is about a quarter of an inch long. They are known as the auditory ossicles and they carry sound from the eardrum to the innermost part of the ear, the cochlea (see pages 154–155).

It's Amazing!

The longest bone is the femur, or thigh bone, which forms one quarter of the body's height. The shortest bone is the stirrup in the ear.

Robert Wadlow in 1938

Oversized Skeleton

The height of the body depends on the size of the skeleton. The tallest person ever, at 9 feet, was Robert Wadlow (1918–1940) of the United States. His thigh bone alone was half the height of a normal adult.

Inside a Bone

A typical bone is not solid. The strongest part is the outer layer, which is called compact bone. Inside this is a layer known as cancellous bone, with holes like a sponge. And inside this, in the middle of the bone, is a soft, jellylike substance called bone marrow.

Lamella

Magnified view of Haversian systems in compact bone

Haversian Systems

Compact bone is made of thousands of tiny rodlike parts called Haversian systems. At the middle of each of these is a hole carrying blood vessels and nerves. Each hole is surrounded by circular layers of bone, called lamellae.

Fibers and Minerals

Bone tissue contains a network of tiny fibers made of a substance called collagen. It also contains hard crystals of the minerals calcium carbonate and calcium phosphate. These crystals are scattered among the collagen fibers. The fibers are flexible and allow the bones to bend slightly, while the minerals make the bones very hard.

Cancellous (spongy) bone

Medullary cavity containing bone marrow

Cutaway view of a typical long bone showing compact bone, cancellous bone, and bone marrow

Compact (hard) bone

Blood vessels

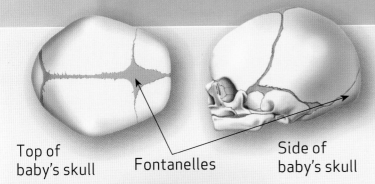

Top of baby's skull   Fontanelles   Side of baby's skull

Holes in the Head

A newborn baby's skull has slight gaps, called fontanelles, between some of its skull bones. These soft areas are pushed together during birth to help the baby's passage through the birth canal.

Inside the Bone

The strands that make up the spongy bone are arranged so that they can absorb the stresses and strains that we put on them as we go through our daily lives. In our longest bones, such as those in our legs, the spongy bone gives way to the medullary cavity, an opening that is full of bone marrow.

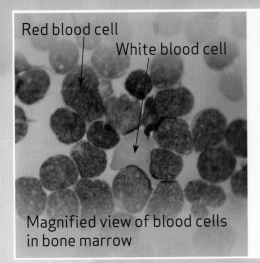

Red blood cell
White blood cell
Magnified view of blood cells in bone marrow

Blood Cells

The bone marrow makes new blood cells (see pages 86–87) to replace old cells that die. The blood cells all start out the same but then change as they develop to form red blood cells, white blood cells, and platelets.

Top Facts

- A human skeleton made of steel would weigh five times more than a real skeleton of bones.

- If bones have to cope regularly with doing more work—for example, by lifting weights—they grow thicker and stronger.

- When we get older, we lose some of the minerals that make up our bones. This can make them brittle and more easily broken than when we are younger.

It's Amazing!

There are about 5 pounds of marrow in an adult's bones. The bone marrow produces more than three million new blood cells every second.

Skull and Spine

The main bone inside the head is the skull. The bones at the front of the skull form the face. Below the skull is the spine, which runs down through the neck, chest, and lower back to the hips.

A mountain biker wears a helmet to protect her head. People who take part in dangerous sports may need to wear extra protection.

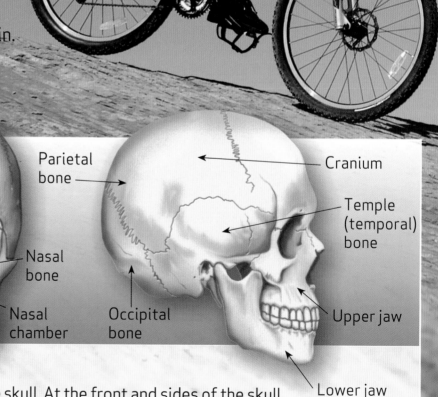

Head Bones

The dome-shaped part of the skull around the brain is called the cranium, and it is made of eight curved bones. Nearly all of the skull bones are joined together, most of them by immovable joints (see page 41). Only one of the bones can move—the mandible, or lower jaw, which forms the chin. It moves at the joints just below each ear.

Forehead (frontal) bone

Parietal bone

Cranium

Eye socket

Temple (temporal) bone

Nasal bone

Cheekbone

Nasal chamber

Occipital bone

Upper jaw

Lower jaw

Face Bones

There are a total of 22 bones in the skull. At the front and sides of the skull are 14 face bones, which give shape to the nose, cheeks, mouth, and chin.

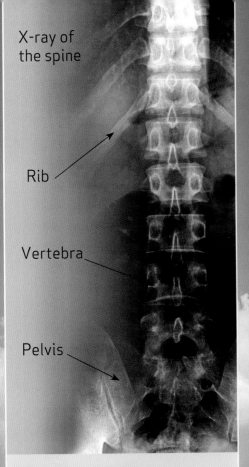

X-ray of
the spine

Rib

Vertebra

Pelvis

Curved and Tube Bones

- Try to bend a flat piece of thin card. It's easy to do.
- Roll the card into a tube shape and hold it in place with some adhesive tape.
- Try to bend the tube. It's much harder to do.
- Many bones are curved, like the skull bones, or tube-shaped, like vertebrae, because it makes them much stronger than if they were flat.

Tower of Bones

The spine is made up of a "tower" of tubelike bones, called vertebrae (as shown in the X-ray above). Each vertebra is separated from its neighbors by a slightly squishy disc.

Main Support

The spine, or backbone, is the body's main central support. It is made up of 24 vertebrae (see left), with 7 in the neck, 12 in the chest, and 5 in the lower back. Below this are two sets of fused bones called the sacrum and the coccyx. Each vertebra can move only slightly against the one next to it, but over the whole backbone these small movements allow the back to bend a long way.

It's Amazing!

Did you know that the human body has a "tail"? The coccyx is a very short, stubby bone at the base of the backbone. However, we cannot see it on the outside.

A woman using a wheelchair because she cannot move her legs

Spinal Injury

Running up the middle of the vertebrae is the spinal cord (see pages 138–139), which is the body's main nerve. Damage to the spinal column can stop the spinal cord carrying messages around the body, which can lead to paralysis, or the inability to move certain limbs.

Connecting Bones

Your bones would fall apart if they were not fastened together by joints. Each joint lets your bones move in a certain direction and by a particular amount. All together, the joints allow your body to move into an amazing variety of positions.

On the Move

Joints are classified by two methods: their structure and the movement they produce. A joint's structure depends upon many different things. These include whether the joint is stuck tightly together to form a suture (see opposite page), or whether it contains cartilage to make the bone movement easier (see page 42).

Types of Joints

In some joints, the ball-shaped end of one bone fits into a bowl-shaped socket in the other bone. These ball-and-socket joints let the bones move back and forth and sideways, and allow them to twist. They are found in the shoulder and hip. In hinge joints, the bones can move back and forth but not sideways. Hinge joints are found in the knees and the finger knuckles.

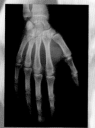

Gliding joints in the hand

Ball-and-socket joint in the hip

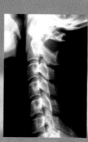

Hinge joint in the knee

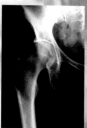

Many joints in the spine

Lots of Joints

Some joints have more than two bones—for example, there are eight bones in the wrist and seven in the ankle. Each of these bones links to those next to it via a gliding joint, in which the bones slide and tilt against each other. The joints in the wrist are flexible, and they allow the hand to move into many positions. The joints in the ankle are less flexible but much stronger, so that they can support the weight of the body.

This gymnast's joints allow her body to move into many different positions.

It's Amazing!

The body's tiniest joint is on the smallest bone, the stirrup, deep inside the ear. The whole joint is smaller than this letter "o."

Top Facts

- There are more than 350 joints in the body.
- The biggest joint is in the knee.
- The most flexible joint is in the shoulder.
- Some joints cannot move at all. These include the joints between the bones in the skull and the joints between the six bones in the hips.

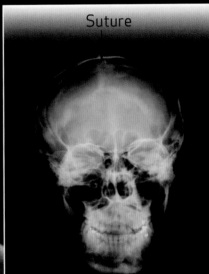

Suture

Skull Joints

An adult's skull bones are joined together with strong fibers set into a kind of glue. These fixed, or immovable, joints look like wavy lines and are known as sutures.

Ready to Throw

Throwing a ball is a good example of how the joints all work together. Just before the ball is released, the joints of the hips, back, shoulder, elbow, wrist, and fingers all move in a fast sequence, one after the other, to hurl the ball at great speed.

A baseball pitcher "winding up" before releasing the ball

Muscles

Almost half of the body is made of muscles. There are hundreds of them, and they power every movement we make. Muscles are actually designed to carry out just one task: to get shorter.

The major skeletal muscles of the body

Skeletal Muscles

Most of the body's muscles are skeletal muscles. These muscles are involved in moving our head, neck, limbs, and torso. They are attached to the bones of the skeleton by tough, ropelike tendons, as opposed to ligaments, which attach the bones to each other. For example, the Achilles tendon attaches the calf muscle to the heel.

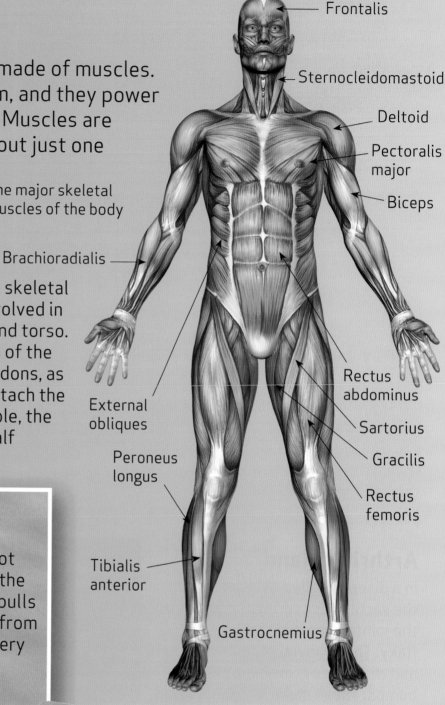

Frontalis

Sternocleidomastoid

Deltoid

Pectoralis major

Biceps

Brachioradialis

Rectus abdominus

External obliques

Sartorius

Gracilis

Peroneus longus

Rectus femoris

Tibialis anterior

Gastrocnemius

It's Amazing!

The smallest muscle is not even as big as this "i." It is the stapedius inside the ear. It pulls the ear bones to stop them from shaking too much during very loud noises.

Biceps

More Muscles?

Bodybuilders who exercise to build up their muscles don't have more muscles than anyone else. Each muscle just becomes bigger and bulges more under the skin.

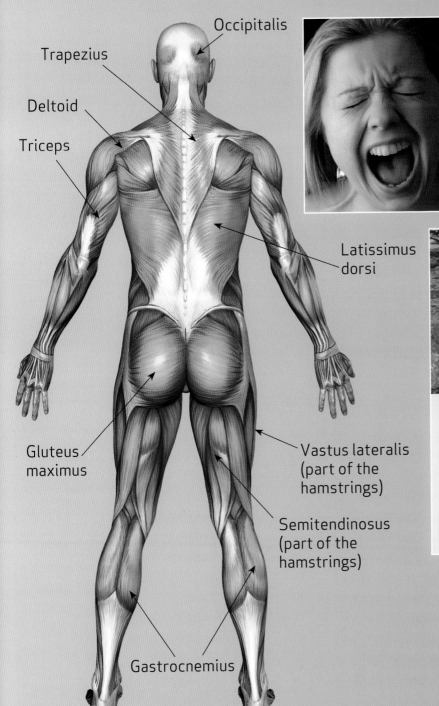

Occipitalis

Trapezius

Deltoid

Triceps

Latissimus dorsi

Gluteus maximus

Vastus lateralis (part of the hamstrings)

Semitendinosus (part of the hamstrings)

Gastrocnemius

Noise Muscles

Your skeletal muscles are also involved in some small, less obvious actions. For example, when you talk or shout, the breathing muscles push out air from the lungs and through the voice box.

Muscle Support

Swimming is especially good for the muscles and joints. It exercises many different muscles at once, and the water supports the body so the joints do not get injured.

Muscle Names

All of the body's muscles have scientific names, and a few of these have become well-known. The pectoralis major muscles, or pectorals, are in the upper chest. The rectus abdominus muscles, or abdominals, are in the front of the abdomen. The biceps are the bulging muscles in the upper arm. Hamstrings is the common name given to the strong muscles at the rear of the thigh.

Top Facts

- The body has about 650 muscles.
- The biggest muscle in the body is the gluteus maximus in the buttock.
- The longest muscle is the sartorius muscle. It runs down the front of the upper leg.

Inside a Muscle

Each muscle is made up of thousands of tiny strands, called muscle fibers, that are about as thick as a hair. The muscles also have blood vessels to bring plenty of blood. The blood carries nutrients, which the muscles use to power their movement.

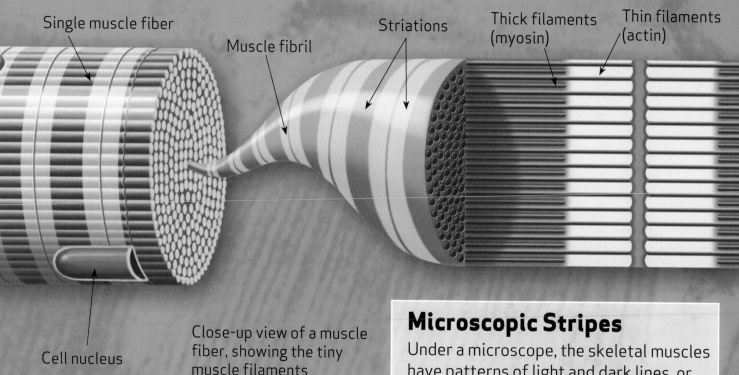

Single muscle fiber

Muscle fibril

Striations

Thick filaments (myosin)

Thin filaments (actin)

Cell nucleus

Close-up view of a muscle fiber, showing the tiny muscle filaments

Smaller and Smaller

There are thousands of muscle fibers in a big muscle, such as the ones in the leg. Each fiber is made of thinner threads, known as muscle fibrils. And each fibril contains even thinner strands, or filaments, of two substances—actin and myosin. These substances are proteins, and they move to make the muscles shorter.

Microscopic Stripes

Under a microscope, the skeletal muscles have patterns of light and dark lines, or striations. These form where groups of thick and thin filaments—myosin and actin—overlap each other.

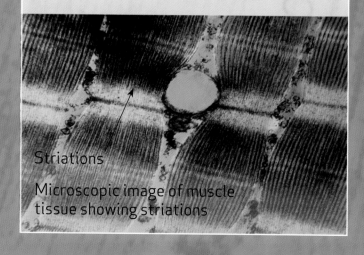

Striations

Microscopic image of muscle tissue showing striations

Sliding Past

A muscle is controlled by nerve signals from the brain. When the signals arrive, they make the strands of actin and myosin slide past each other. As they do so, they shorten the fibril, which in turn shortens the fiber and the whole muscle. Most muscles can shorten to about two-thirds of their relaxed length.

It's Amazing!

The body's most flexible muscle is the one you use to talk, eat, drink, and lick your lips.
It's your tongue!

In this tug-of-war game, the muscles in the arms and legs stay the same length rather than getting shorter.

Taking the Strain

Muscles can also work by generating tension, which stops the muscle length changing, allowing you to pull against something else. This type of muscle use is called isometric, which means "same length."

Playing video games too much can result in RSI of the hands

Wear and Tear

Muscles, tendons, nerves, and joints that repeat the same movement may suffer damage. This can result in pain known as RSI, or repetitive strain injury. RSI happens most commonly in the hands—often in the hand used to control a computer mouse.

Finger Control

- Hold out your hand with your fingers together and straight.
- Then, curl your fingers all at the same time, as though you are gripping something.
- Now, try to curl each finger on its own, while keeping the others straight.
- It's harder to curl one finger at a time, because your brain has to learn to send the correct nerve signals to control the muscles in each finger.

How Muscles Work

Every movement needs muscles—not just jumping or lifting something heavy, but simple actions that we do all the time, such as blinking and breathing.

Shorten and Stretch

A muscle can pull, but it cannot push. This means that a single muscle can only move a bone in one direction. Another muscle is needed in order to pull a bone in the opposite direction. Many muscles are arranged as opposite partners, working together to pull bones one way and then the other.

Muscle Matters

- The word "muscle" comes from the Latin word *musculus*, meaning "little mouse," because in the past people thought that bulging muscles looked like a mouse running under the skin!
- The first accurate pictures of the whole muscle system were drawn by the artist and scientist Andreas Vesalius in 1543.

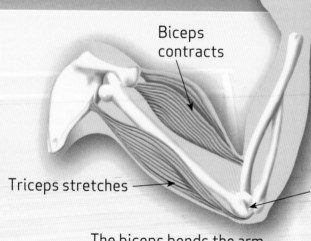

Biceps contracts

Triceps stretches

Elbow bends

The biceps bends the arm.

Triceps contracts

Biceps stretches

The triceps straightens the arm.

Elbow straightens

Opposing Partners

The main muscles in the upper arm are the biceps and triceps. When the biceps contracts, it pulls the lower arm up. This makes the elbow bend because the triceps is relaxed. When the triceps contracts, or gets shorter, it pulls the lower arm down. This straightens the elbow and stretches the biceps. The triceps and biceps are examples of muscles that work as antagonistic, or opposing, partners.

Working Together

Aside from very simple actions such as blinking, few movements use just one or two muscles. As you write your name, your finger muscles hold the pen, and your hand and wrist muscles move the pen to form the words. Your arm and shoulder muscles move your whole arm along the page, and your eye, head, and neck muscles move so you can watch what you write. More than 100 muscles are involved!

A crane uses cables to pull and lift heavy loads.

Pulling Force

A crane's lifting cable works similarly to a muscle. It lifts the load, or pulls it up, by shortening the cable as it winds onto a spool.

It's Amazing!

The widest muscles in your body are the external obliques, which run from the middle of your back and around to your stomach. They can be up to 18 inches wide.

Using Muscles

Learning to use muscles together can take a lot of time. Movements that you find easy today, such as walking, may have taken you 12 months to learn as a baby.

A ballet dancer using the muscles in her legs to stand *en pointe*, or on tiptoe

Other Types of Muscle

The skeletal muscles are not the body's only muscles. The heart has its own type of muscle, and the gut, blood vessels, and many other parts have a kind of muscle called smooth muscle.

Cardiac Muscle

If we use some muscles too much, they become tired and weak, but one type of muscle never tires. It is the cardiac muscle that makes up the walls of the heart, and it works every second of every day to pump blood around the body. The walls of the blood vessels contain smooth muscles, which alter the width of these tubes to control how much blood flows to different body parts.

It's Amazing!

Usually the muscles in the stomach and gut work smoothly, but if we get startled or feel worried these muscles can suddenly shorten. We feel this as a fluttering—known as butterflies—in our stomach.

Top Facts

Smooth muscles are found in the walls of many parts of the body, including:

- The esophagus, or food pipe.
- The stomach.
- The intestines.
- The blood vessels.
- The windpipe.
- The airways in the lungs called bronchi and bronchioles (see pages 66–67).
- The ureters—the tubes that carry urine from the kidneys to the bladder.
- The bladder.

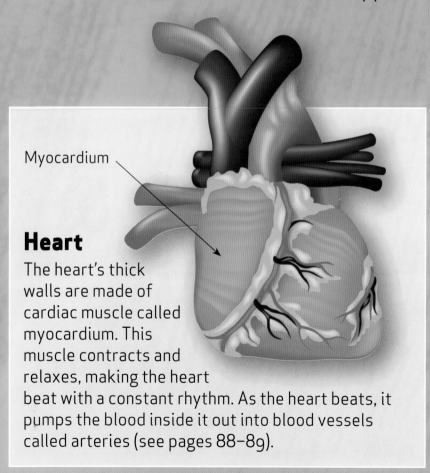

Myocardium

Heart

The heart's thick walls are made of cardiac muscle called myocardium. This muscle contracts and relaxes, making the heart beat with a constant rhythm. As the heart beats, it pumps the blood inside it out into blood vessels called arteries (see pages 88–89).

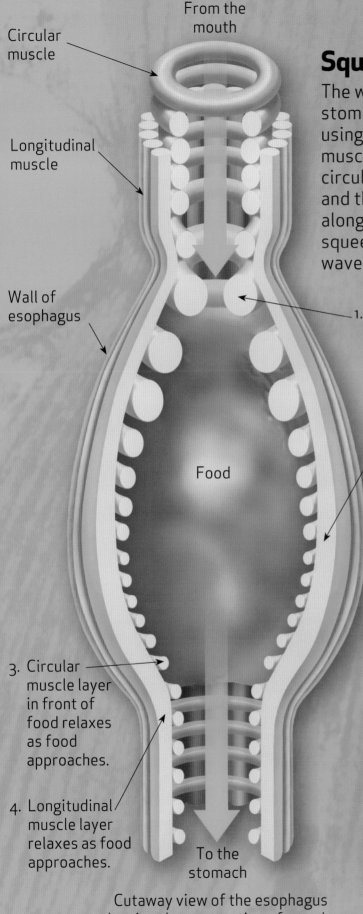

Circular muscle

From the mouth

Longitudinal muscle

Wall of esophagus

Food

3. Circular muscle layer in front of food relaxes as food approaches.

4. Longitudinal muscle layer relaxes as food approaches.

To the stomach

Cutaway view of the esophagus showing the contraction of muscles during peristalsis

Squeezing Food

The walls of the gut—the esophagus, stomach, and intestines—push food along using smooth muscles. These smooth muscles are arranged in two directions. The circular muscles form rings around the gut and the longitudinal muscles run lengthways along the gut. These layers work together to squeeze the food through the gut using a wave action called peristalsis.

1. Circular muscle layer behind food contracts to push food forward.

2. Longitudinal muscle layer contracts to shorten tube.

Automatic Journey

We bite, chew, and swallow using muscles in the face and neck that we control. Once the food gets into the esophagus, the automatic movements of the smooth muscles take food down into the stomach and through the intestines (see pages 104–105).

Bone, Joint, and Muscle Problems

Overexerting ourselves or putting too much pressure on our bones, joints, and muscles can cause breaks, strains, or tears that may require medical treatment.

Muscle Cramp

Sometimes, muscles experience an uncontrolled contraction, or tightening, known as a cramp. This often happens during exercise, when a chemical called lactic acid builds up in the muscles. It can also be caused by a lack of certain minerals, such as potassium.

The soccer player on the ground has developed a cramp, so his teammate is stretching his legs to relieve the pain.

Top Facts

- A muscle strain is when a muscle pulls too hard and damages some of its fibers.

- A muscle tear is like a strain but the muscle fibers split.

- A joint sprain is when a joint moves too far and its parts become swollen, stiff, and painful.

New Hip

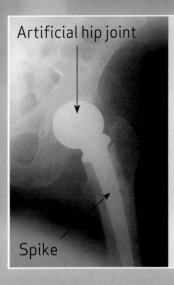

Artificial hip joint

Spike

This X-ray shows an artificial hip joint (see page 43). The ball-shaped end of the thigh bone has been replaced with a metal one and fixed into the thigh bone with a spike.

Breaks

A break in a bone is called a fracture. It may be a slight crack or a complete snap. An X-ray tells the doctor if the bone is fractured. If it is, the doctor may push the broken bone back together. The bone may be held in place by a plaster or fiberglass cast as it heals.

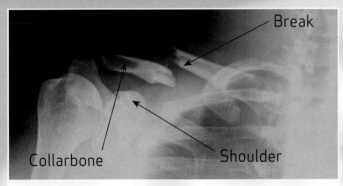

Break

Collarbone

Shoulder

Broken Collarbone

A broken collarbone, as shown in this X-ray, is often caused by falling and putting an arm straight out to prevent the head from hitting the ground. The force of the fall passes from the arm to the shoulder and snaps the collarbone.

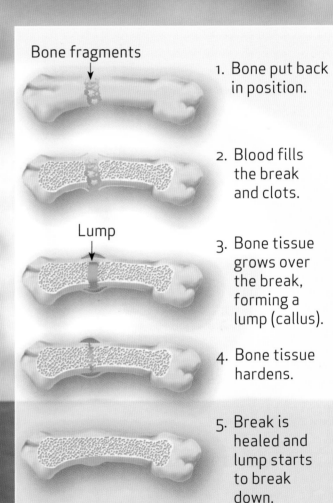

Bone fragments

Lump

1. Bone put back in position.

2. Blood fills the break and clots.

3. Bone tissue grows over the break, forming a lump (callus).

4. Bone tissue hardens.

5. Break is healed and lump starts to break down.

Healing a Break

The body takes about six weeks to repair a broken bone, depending on how bad the break is. Blood fills the break and new bone tissue grows in the gap. This gradually hardens to form a permanent, strong repair.

Healthy Bones and Joints

Bones, joints, and muscles are meant to be used, and exercise can help them to stay healthy. You should also eat a good diet so that these body parts can stay strong and active, and repair themselves if they get damaged.

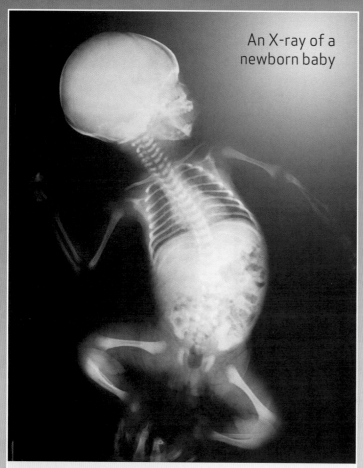

An X-ray of a newborn baby

Keeping Active

We need to use our bones, joints, and muscles often or they will weaken and waste away. In addition to sports, there are helpful things we can do as part of our daily lives. We can walk or cycle rather than travel by car, and use the stairs rather than elevators— all of these small actions combine to keep our bodies healthy.

Baby Skeleton

As a baby develops in the womb, its skeleton first forms from cartilage. The cartilage gradually turns into bone, and this process—known as ossification— continues during childhood. The whole skeleton is not fully grown, mature, and hardened until a person has reached about 20 years of age.

It's Amazing!

Improvements in muscle training methods and diet mean that a modern champion runner can finish the 100-meter sprint almost one second faster than a champion runner of 100 years ago.

Warm up, Cool Down

Sports people and athletes know the importance of proper training. If the body tries to do too much too quickly, it can suffer injuries, such as sprains and strains. Before you start exercising, it's important to get expert advice. You should also do warm-up exercises, such as bending and stretching, before a sudden burst of activity. Then, do cool-down exercises afterward to help the body relax again.

Healthy Bones

Bones and teeth contain large amounts of the mineral calcium. Milk and other dairy products are rich in calcium. If they are consumed during childhood, they help the bones and teeth to grow healthy and strong.

This runner is stretching her leg muscles before exercising.

Top Facts

- Some people are naturally fitter and better at sports and exercise than other people. You should aim to improve your own performance rather than try to match someone else's.

- You should exercise steadily and get advice from a coach.

- It is important to have the correct equipment, especially footwear.

- You should wear the correct body protection and pads for contact sports, such as football.

LUNGS AND BREATHING

In an emergency, your body can get by without food for several days, and it can even cope without water for a day or so. But one thing is so vital that your body cannot survive more than a few minutes without it—the gas oxygen. You take in oxygen from the air around you by breathing, using the parts of the body called the respiratory system. You don't have to think about breathing—your body does it automatically—but it keeps you alive.

The Breathing System

The respiratory, or breathing, system is located in the head, neck, and chest. You use it to draw air deep into your lungs. Here, oxygen passes into the blood and then spreads all around your body.

Bigger and Smaller

The lungs act like two balloons inside your chest. As you draw air into the breathing system (see pages 68–69), the lungs get bigger as they fill with air. Then, when you breathe out, air is pushed out of the lungs and they get smaller.

The Airways

The upper airways in the head and neck include the nasal chamber in the nose (see page 60) and the throat. The lower airways include the windpipe in the neck and the tubes called bronchi and bronchioles, which carry air into the lungs. At the top of the windpipe is the larynx, or voice box, which produces the voice when air passes through it.

The main parts of the respiratory system in the neck and chest

Voice box (larynx)

Windpipe (trachea)

Left lung

Right lung

Upper lobe

Upper lobe

Main airway (bronchus)

Middle lobe

Lower lobe

Lower lobe

Smaller airways (bronchioles)

Fanning the Flames

In ancient times, many people thought that body warmth came from food being burned in the heart. They believed that breathing was a way of providing air for the burning flames in the heart. They thought that when the body was active, breathing increased to provide more air to fan the flames, which made the body hotter.

Down Into the Lungs

The breathing muscles create the movement that sucks air in and pushes air out of your lungs. The most important muscles are the dome-shaped diaphragm below the lungs and the long muscles between the ribs called intercostals. The backbone, ribs, and breastbone form a cage around the lungs, which protects these parts yet still allows the breathing action (see pages 68–69).

It's Amazing!

A free diver is someone who dives underwater without an air tank. Some free divers can hold their breath for more than six minutes when they dive.

Sense of Smell

Air coming in through the nose carries tiny particles of smell chemicals. These particles land on sensitive patches in the roof of the nasal chamber. The patches figure out the type of particle and send information about the smell to the brain (see pages 156–157).

Blowing

In normal breathing, air flows in and out through the nose, but the airflow can be directed out through the mouth. This is useful for all kinds of actions, from blowing out candles to playing the trumpet.

Inside the Nose

At rest, most air is breathed in through the nose. Inside the nose, air is cleaned, warmed, and moistened to make it more suitable for traveling into the lungs. Dusty, cold, or dry air can clog the lungs or dry out the airways.

Air Filters

The nose is separated into two nostrils by a wall of cartilage. The nostrils have small hairs inside them that catch bits of dust and other particles floating in the air. The nostrils are the entrance to the nasal cavity, an air-filled space that works like an air filter. The lining of the nasal cavity is coated with a layer of mucus, a thick, sticky fluid that moistens the air and traps germs, dust, and other particles.

An X-ray of the skull showing the nasal cavity and the sinuses

Frontal sinus

Ethmoid and sphenoid sinuses

Maxillary sinus

Nasal cavity

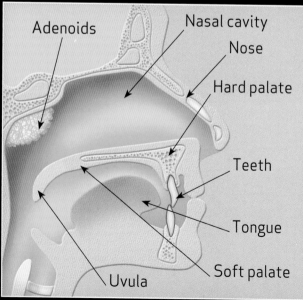

Adenoids

Nasal cavity

Nose

Hard palate

Teeth

Tongue

Soft palate

Uvula

Nasal Cavity

The nasal cavity is separated from the mouth by the palate, which is divided into the hard, bony palate at the front and the soft palate at the back. The adenoids are bulges of tissue that help to trap and remove germs from the air.

Eye socket

Top Facts

- Branching off the nasal cavity are a number of air-filled spaces called sinuses.

- There are four sets of sinuses in the skull. These are the frontal, ethmoid, sphenoid, and maxillary sinuses.

- No one knows exactly what the sinuses are for, but they may be used to help make the different sounds of speech, or to help with temperature control within the head, or to make the bones of the skull lighter.

Synchronized swimmers wearing nose clips

Closed Nose

Synchronized swimmers usually wear a nose clip when they are performing. This stops water entering the nasal cavity and irritating the cavity lining, especially when the swimmers are upside down in the pool.

Warmed by Blood

The nasal cavity has a thin lining with a network of blood vessels just beneath the surface. The warm blood flowing through these vessels gives out heat to the passing air, warming the air. These blood vessels are delicate—a blow to the nose may break one and cause a nosebleed.

Face Masks

People with certain jobs, such as builders and miners, wear masks with filters. These masks stop dust particles (which the nasal cavity cannot trap) from entering the breathing system, where they might cause damage.

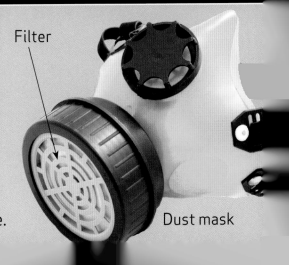
Filter

Dust mask

In the Throat

The throat has two functions—it is a passageway for air and for food. Swallowing closes off the windpipe, so food is not accidentally carried into the lower airways.

The Right Way

When you swallow, the entrance to the windpipe tilts up and forward and a stiff flap—the epiglottis—tilts down over it. This piece of cartilage blocks the upper entrance to your windpipe, which means that food slides down into the esophagus. It is not possible to breathe when swallowing because the windpipe is closed.

When we eat, we do not usually think about the action of swallowing—we just do it.

It's Amazing!

On average, a person swallows 300 times during a meal and up to 2,000 times during a whole day.

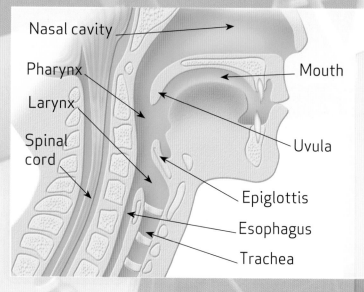

Nasal cavity

Pharynx

Larynx

Spinal cord

Mouth

Uvula

Epiglottis

Esophagus

Trachea

Open Wide

The throat connects your mouth and nasal cavity to your trachea, or windpipe, and the esophagus, which is a tube down to the stomach. The upper part of the throat is called the pharynx. Below this is the larynx, or voice box, which is the opening to the respiratory tract. At the sides of the throat there are bulges of special germ-killing tissue called the tonsils, which, like the adenoids, help to fight infection.

Swollen Tonsils

The tonsils may swell when they are fighting germs in the body, causing a sore throat and discomfort when swallowing. This illness is called tonsillitis.

Tonsils

A child with infected tonsils

The Wrong Way

Very rarely, swallowed food may go down "the wrong way." This means it goes into the windpipe and blocks the airway. If this happens, breathing becomes difficult and can even stop, causing choking. Usually a cough removes the blockage by forcing fast-moving air up from the lungs. This pushes the food up into the throat for safe swallowing.

Choking

If coughing cannot remove an obstruction from the windpipe, then a trained person may have to perform the Heimlich maneuver. This other person squeezes the abdomen to press the lungs, which forces air and the blockage out.

Lower Airways

The lower airways carry breathed-in air down through the neck and into the lungs. There, the airways divide many times, becoming smaller and smaller as they carry air into the deepest parts of the lungs.

Airway Tree

The system of branching airways is often compared to an upside-down tree. The main "trunk" is the trachea, or windpipe. This divides into two main airway "branches," the left bronchus and right bronchus. These bronchi split over and over again. They first form secondary bronchi, and then split to become smaller and smaller until they eventually become the smallest airways, known as bronchioles, which are the tree's "twigs" (see pages 66–67).

Top Facts

- An average adult's windpipe is about 5 inches long. Inside, it is about half an inch wide.

- When we breathe in deeply or crane our neck to look up and forward, the windpipe can stretch in length by up to 1 inch.

Voice box (larynx)

Cartilage rings

Windpipe (trachea)

Right bronchus

Right secondary bronchi

Left bronchus

Left secondary bronchi

The Windpipe

The windpipe starts at the base of the larynx, or voice box. Its walls are formed by 16 to 20 C-shaped rings of cartilage. These allow the windpipe to stretch, twist, and shorten as the neck moves, yet remain open for air to flow through it.

Trachea

Esophagus

Inside the Trachea

The trachea and the esophagus run side by side down the neck (see main image). The C-shaped rings of cartilage that surround the trachea allow it to squish slightly if a large piece of food passes down the esophagus.

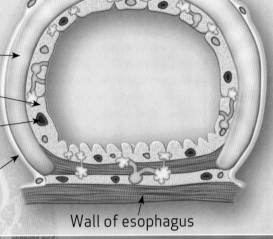

Cartilage C-ring

Lining of trachea

Small artery

Outer wall

Wall of esophagus

It's Amazing!

In a baby, the diameter of the windpipe is very small—about an eighth of an inch. This is not much wider than the ink tube inside a typical ballpoint pen.

Keeping Clean

The windpipe and other airways are lined with a sticky fluid called mucus, or phlegm. This traps germs and bits of dirt floating in the breathed-in air. The mucus is made by microscopic cells called goblet cells in the airway lining. Coughing brings mucus up from the airways into the throat, where it can be swallowed (see page 71).

Cilia on the lining of the airway

Tiny Hairs

Microscopic hairs called cilia stick out from the lining of the airways. They wave continuously to push mucus up the airways.

Deep in the Lungs

The lungs are like elastic bags filled with millions of tiny balloons. In each lung, the branching airways become thinner and shorter until, finally, after about 15 divisions from the windpipe, they are narrower than human hairs.

The Lungs

Each lung is made up of sections called lobes (see page 58), and each lobe has a bronchus leading to it. The right lung has three lobes—upper, middle, and lower. The left lung is smaller and has only two lobes—upper and lower—because it has a scooped-out area where the heart sits. The esophagus and the main blood vessels lie between the lungs.

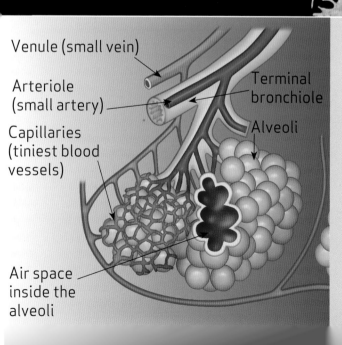

Venule (small vein)

Arteriole (small artery)

Capillaries (tiniest blood vessels)

Terminal bronchiole

Alveoli

Air space inside the alveoli

Into the Blood

The smallest airways, called the terminal bronchioles, carry air to groups of microscopic, bubble-shaped air sacs called alveoli. The alveoli are surrounded by plenty of blood vessels so that oxygen can pass easily from the lungs and into the blood.

A resin cast showing the smaller and smaller airways inside the lungs

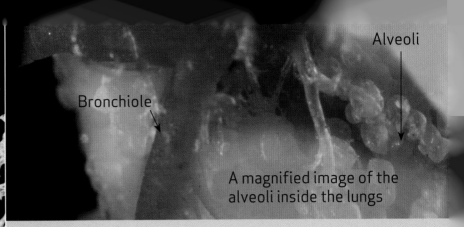

Bronchiole

Alveoli

A magnified image of the alveoli inside the lungs

Top Facts

- Each lung has about 300 million alveoli.
- Each alveolus is about 0.008 inches in diameter.
- The name "alveolus" comes from the Latin word meaning "little cavity."
- If spread out, the millions of alveoli in a pair of lungs would cover an area the size of a tennis court.

Alveoli

Under a microscope, alveoli look like small, almost see-through balloons. Most alveoli are not separate from each other but are squished together so that they look like bunches of grapes. As a result of this, they are partly merged inside and have one large, shared air space.

Into the Blood

Oxygen from breathed-in air passes into the body through the alveoli. It seeps from the air in the alveoli into the blood in the microscopic blood vessels, known as capillaries, around the alveoli. This is also where carbon dioxide, a gas we produce, moves from the blood into the alveoli and is eventually breathed out.

It's Amazing!

The lungs can also help us to float. In fact, people float more easily on water if they breathe in deeply and then take small breaths, keeping the lungs as full of air as possible.

Movements of Breathing

The actions of the main breathing muscles—the intercostals and the diaphragm—are carried out automatically. As a result, you do not have to think about breathing in and out for most of the time.

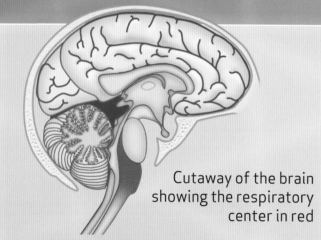

Cutaway of the brain showing the respiratory center in red

Breathing Control

The breathing muscles are controlled by signals from a part of the brain called the respiratory center. Sensors detect the amounts of oxygen and carbon dioxide in the blood. As carbon dioxide levels rise and oxygen levels fall, the brain tells the breathing muscles to work harder.

Breathing In

To inhale, or breathe in, the diaphragm contracts, becoming flatter. This pulls the lungs downward. At the same time, the intercostals contract and make the ribs move up and out. The result is that the lungs are stretched and suck air in through the nose and down the windpipe into the chest.

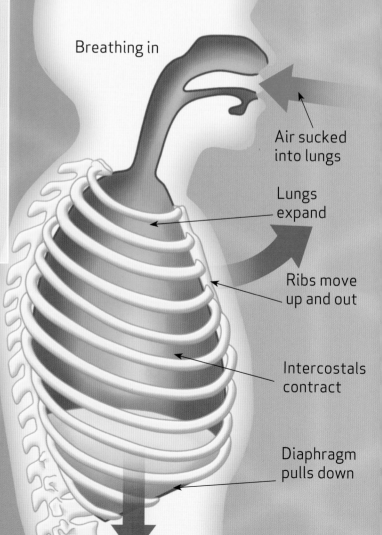

Breathing in

Air sucked into lungs

Lungs expand

Ribs move up and out

Intercostals contract

Diaphragm pulls down

Breathing Rate

- Rest for a few minutes, then count how many breaths you take in 1 minute. Then jog in place for 3 minutes, and count your breaths.

- Rest again, then count your breaths. Your breathing rate should rise after activity, then gradually return to its resting rate.

A boy holding his breath while he jumps into water

Breathing Out

To exhale, or breathe out, the diaphragm and the intercostals all relax. The lungs, which have stretched like a balloon, spring back to their usual shape. This makes the diaphragm return to its dome shape and the ribs move down and in. As the lungs shrink, they push air up the windpipe and out through the nose.

Stop Breathing

We have to make ourselves stop breathing when we jump into water. The brain tries to make us breathe, but we can prevent it for a while so our lungs are not filled with water.

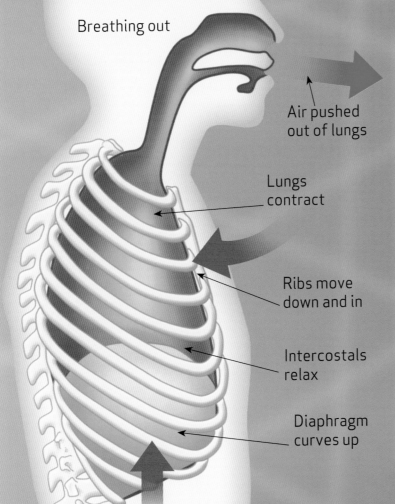

Breathing out

Air pushed out of lungs

Lungs contract

Ribs move down and in

Intercostals relax

Diaphragm curves up

Mouth-to-Mouth

Breathed-out air still contains some oxygen. It can be blown into someone's lungs in an emergency if he or she has stopped breathing. This is called artificial respiration.

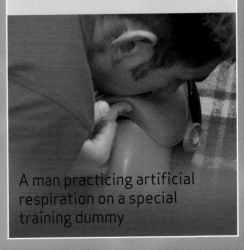

A man practicing artificial respiration on a special training dummy

Coughs and Sneezes

Potentially harmful substances in the air are sometimes breathed into the lungs. Fortunately, the body has ways of protecting itself from these foreign invaders, and can get rid of them at superfast speeds.

Sneezing

Small particles of dust that get into the nose may irritate the nose lining. This produces the sneeze reflex. Muscles in the chest, the diaphragm (see pages 68–69), and the throat contract—or get smaller—very quickly. This forces air up through the nose, carrying the cause of the irritation and mucus out with it.

Top Facts

- You always close your eyes when you sneeze.

- A typical sneeze will blow about 40,000 tiny droplets of mucus and saliva out of the nose and mouth.

- The droplets blown out by coughs and sneezes may contain germs. This is why it is important to cover your mouth and nose.

Sneezing can be caused by tiny plant particles called pollen. This is known as hay fever (see page 74).

Airway Irritation

If an irritation occurs lower down the breathing system, such as in the trachea or the lungs, then the body produces a cough to clear it. The irritation may be caused by small particles of dust, or it might be caused by an illness that inflames the linings of the lower airways.

Always put your hand over your mouth when coughing, to stop the spread of germs.

Coughing

To cope with an irritation in the airways, the lining of the breathing passages produces excessive mucus. The body coughs to get rid of this excessive mucus. As with a sneeze, a cough is caused by a sudden contraction of the muscles in the chest, which forces air, as well as the excess mucus and the cause of the irritation, out of the lungs.

A firefighter wearing breathing apparatus

Dust and Smoke Protection

People who work in dusty or smoky places need to wear protection to stop dangerous particles from entering the breathing system. In some cases, this protection can be a simple mask, which blocks larger dust particles (see page 61). However, in very smoky environments, such as a fire, a person may need to carry a supply of dust-free air.

It's Amazing!

Sneezes blow air out of the nose at speeds of up to 93 miles per hour!

Nose and Throat Problems

Breathing difficulties may be caused by physical problems with the structure of the respiratory, or breathing, system. This can lead to a variety of conditions, such as snoring.

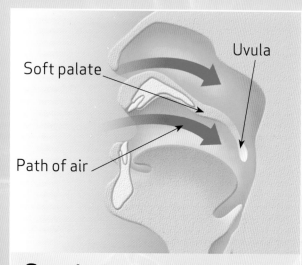

Soft palate

Uvula

Path of air

Snoring

Snoring is caused by the vibration of soft parts at the back of the throat, such as the soft palate and the flap that hangs down at the back of the mouth, called the uvula. These parts vibrate as air passes over them when a person is asleep. This noisy vibration can keep other people awake. Snoring can be caused by a variety of conditions, such as fat gathering around the throat, a blockage of the nose passages, or a weakness of the throat muscles.

A magnified view of an influenza virus

Dangerous Substances

The respiratory system can be damaged by substances in the air. These can include tiny organisms, such as viruses and germs that cause illnesses like colds and influenza. They can also be chemicals that the body cannot get rid of by coughing and that can damage the body's tissues.

It's Amazing!

The loudest recorded snore measured 93 decibels—that's louder than the sound of a pneumatic drill breaking up concrete.

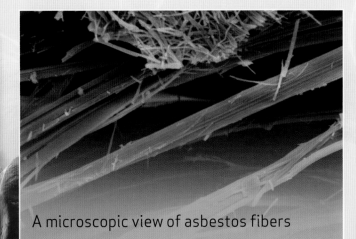

A microscopic view of asbestos fibers

Asbestos

Asbestos is a flame-resistant material that was used in buildings until the 1980s. It was then discovered that the tiny strands that make up some kinds of asbestos could cause cancer when breathed in. As a result, asbestos is banned in many countries, and any found in old buildings has to be disposed of very carefully.

Smog

Smog is a cloud of potentially harmful gas that is formed when sunlight reacts with polluting gases from car exhausts and factories. Smog can cause soreness and irritation in the nose and throat, as well as breathing problems like asthma.

Smog hangs over the city of Los Angeles, California.

Allergies and Lung Problems

Breathing problems lower down in the respiratory system may be caused by issues with the organs themselves, or by an overly protective reaction by the body, which is known as an allergy.

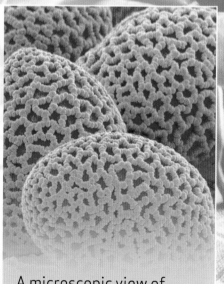

It's Amazing!

A single person sheds one-twentieth of an ounce of skin cells every day. That is enough to feed up to a million dust mites.

Too Protective?

Allergic reactions are the body's response to allergens, or foreign substances—even though these substances might be harmless. When the body detects an allergen, it triggers the release of chemicals, which start a sequence of reactions designed to protect the body. Some of these reactions, however—such as a runny nose and sneezing—can be a nuisance, while others can be dangerous.

Hay Fever

Hay fever is an allergic response that is triggered by tiny pollen grains. These grains are produced by plants in spring and summer. When the pollen grains are breathed in, they cause the body to release a chemical called histamine. This chemical irritates the linings of the breathing system, causing a runny nose and sneezing.

A microscopic view of pollen grains

Top Facts

• Some allergic reactions are treated using drugs called antihistamines, which stop the production of histamine.

• The name "asthma" comes from a Greek word meaning "sharp breath."

Breathing Conditions

Many people suffer from conditions that make breathing difficult. Some of these conditions are inherited, or passed on, from parents. They include cystic fibrosis, which causes a build-up of extra-thick mucus in the lungs, sinus infections, poor growth, and a weak immune system (see pages 96–97).

A young boy is massaged while wearing a device called a mask nebulizer as part of his treatment for cystic fibrosis

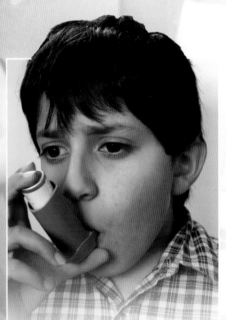

A boy using an inhaler to treat asthma

Tiny Creatures

Dust mites are tiny creatures that feed on the dust found in our homes and workplaces. The waste products they leave behind are a major cause of allergic responses in many people, such as asthma (see right).

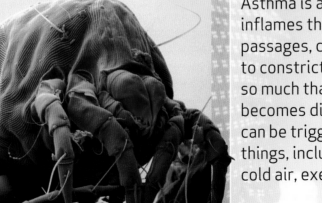

A microscopic view of a dust mite

Asthma

Asthma is a condition that inflames the breathing passages, causing them to constrict, or narrow, so much that breathing becomes difficult. Asthma can be triggered by many things, including allergens, cold air, exercise, or stress.

Keeping Airways and Lungs Healthy

Keeping the airways clear and healthy is vital for our well-being. Getting oxygen into our bodies is essential, and any reduction in the amount of this gas could have disastrous consequences.

A cyclist wearing a mask to reduce the amount of traffic fumes he inhales

Deep Breath

As with any muscles, the intercostal muscles and the diaphragm (see pages 68–69) benefit from regular exercise. This helps to make them stronger and to improve your breathing system.

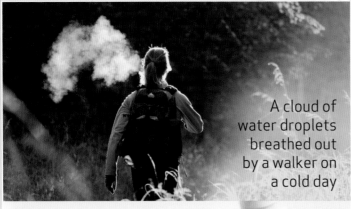

A cloud of water droplets breathed out by a walker on a cold day

Moisture in Breath

The air you breathe out contains more water vapor than the air you breathe in—you can see a cloud of water vapor when you breathe out on a cold day. This highlights one of the ways in which the body loses water (see pages 122–123). It is important that we do not lose too much water. We need to drink plenty of liquids to replace it.

It's Amazing!

The average person breathes about 21,600 times every day. This draws about 2,000 gallons of air into the lungs every 24 hours.

Keeping Fit

Exercise is important for keeping the breathing system healthy. Long periods of exercise, called cardiovascular exercise, include walking, running, cycling, and swimming. This type of exercise gets you breathing harder than normal, which exercises the muscles involved in breathing and makes them stronger.

Going for a long walk or run can improve your breathing system

Water in Breath

- Place a small mirror in the fridge for an hour.

- Take the mirror out and then breathe out over it.

- You will see that the mirror fogs up where you breathe on it. This fog on the mirror is caused by the water vapor in the air you breathe out.

Keeping Bad Stuff Out

Every day, you breathe in substances that are bad for your body. Most of the time, your body can get rid of these using a variety of actions, such as coughing and sneezing. Exposure to excessive amounts of bad chemicals, however, such as cigarette smoke and traffic fumes, can have dangerous effects, including lung diseases and cancer.

Even if you don't smoke, breathing in another person's cigarette smoke can be dangerous.

Smoking

Smoking is bad for the breathing system. The smoke strips away the cilia from the linings of the airways, making it hard to remove excess mucus and potentially dangerous substances. The smoke also contains more than 4,000 chemicals, 69 of which are known to cause cancer.

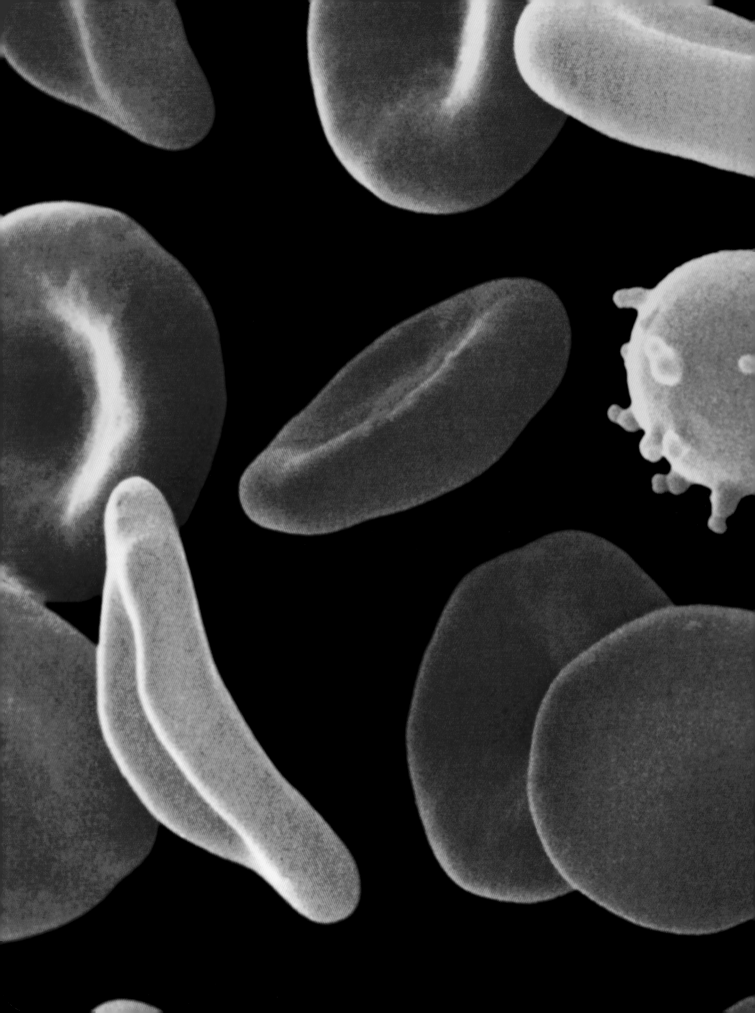

HEART AND BLOOD

The heart is an amazing pump that works nonstop to keep the body alive. With every beat it sends a surge of blood carrying vital supplies, such as oxygen, and the body's waste products, such as carbon dioxide, through a network of blood vessels to and from every part of the body. The heart, blood, and vessels are together known as the circulatory, or cardiovascular, system.

Nonstop Pump

The heart is a muscular pump that works constantly to squeeze blood into blood vessels called arteries. The arteries take the blood around the body, and the veins return the blood to the heart.

The mechanical pump of a fountain uses force to squirt water a great distance.

Powerful Pump

Just like a fountain forces water out, the heart muscle contracts to push blood at great force into the arteries. Your heart will do this about two and a half billion times during your life.

The Right Pump

The heart is really two pumps side by side. The right pump sends blood along the pulmonary arteries to the lungs, where it absorbs oxygen. This blood then comes back along the pulmonary veins to the left side of the heart to be pumped around the rest of the body (see right).

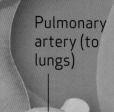

Superior vena cava (main vein from upper body)

Arteries to upper body, neck, and head

Pulmonary veins (from lungs)

Aorta (main artery to body)

Pulmonary artery (to lungs)

Coronary arteries

Right side of heart

Inferior vena cava (main vein from lower body)

Artery to lower body and legs

Muscle of heart wall

Left side of heart

A view of the outside of the heart and main blood vessels

Valves stop blood from flowing the wrong way in the veins.

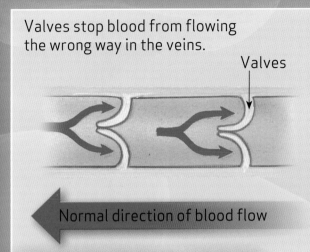

Valves

Normal direction of blood flow

Studying Veins

The veins are just under the skin in some places, and can be seen as dark lines. The blood in the veins does not flow with as much pressure as the blood being forced through the arteries by the heart. Because vein blood flows with a lower pressure, there is a risk that it could flow the wrong way. To stop this, the larger veins have valves in them, and these slam shut to stop blood from flowing the wrong way.

It's Amazing!

With each pump, blood surges out into the main arteries at a speed of 15 inches per second. If it were to pass through a hole the size of a pinhead at this speed and pressure, it would spurt more than 10 feet.

The Left Pump

The left side of the heart is larger and more powerful than the right side. While the right side of the heart pumps blood to the lungs, the left side pumps blood all around the body, delivering oxygen, energy, and nutrients from food to every part. Then the blood, which is now low in oxygen, returns from all of these body parts along the veins to the heart's right side. There, it begins its nonstop journey back to the lungs and then around the body once again.

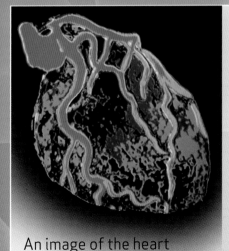

An image of the heart with the coronary arteries shown in red

Blood Supply

The heart muscle has its own blood supply—the coronary arteries. Blood flows along these arteries into the heart muscle and then out along the coronary veins. If the coronary arteries become blocked, the heart muscle may die. This is one form of a heart attack.

Harvey's Discovery

For centuries, people believed that blood flowed into the body, where it was used up. In 1628, English physician William Harvey did experiments that showed that blood circulates around and around the body in the blood vessels, returning to the heart at the end of each circuit.

Inside the Heart

The heart is not a solid lump of muscle but has four inner compartments, called chambers. Blood flows through these chambers, with four valves, or flaps, making sure that it flows the right way.

The yellow arrows show the passage of blood through the heart as it is pumped to and from the lungs and body.

Upper Chambers

Each half of the heart has an upper chamber, which is called an atrium. The left atrium receives blood from the lungs. The right atrium takes in blood from the body.

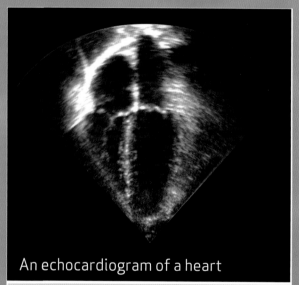

An echocardiogram of a heart

Echocardiogram

Sound waves can be beamed into the heart, where they hit different parts and echo back. These echoes form a moving picture called an echocardiogram, which shows the four chambers of the heart.

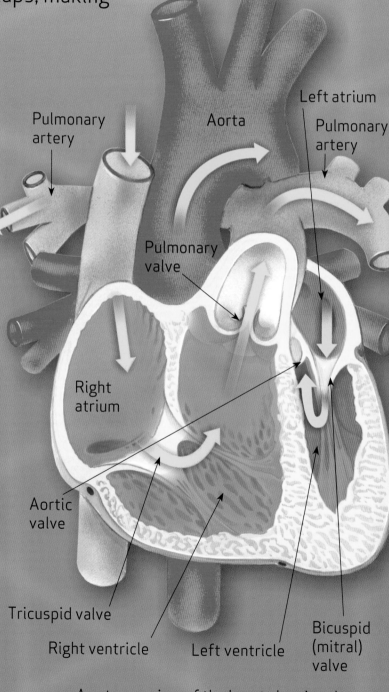

Pulmonary artery

Aorta

Left atrium

Pulmonary artery

Pulmonary valve

Right atrium

Aortic valve

Tricuspid valve

Right ventricle

Left ventricle

Bicuspid (mitral) valve

A cutaway view of the heart showing the four chambers and the valves inside

It's Amazing!

During a typical day, the adult heart pumps out about 2,000 gallons of blood. That would be enough blood to fill more than 50 baths.

Lower Chambers

Each side of the heart also has a lower chamber, which is called a ventricle. Each ventricle receives blood from the atrium above it through a funnel-shaped valve. As the ventricles squeeze, they push blood out through one-way valves into the main arteries.

Top Facts

- In a typical adult at rest, the heart pumps about 70 times each minute and sends out about 5 tablespoons of blood with each beat.

- The heart pumps about 1.5 gallons of blood each minute, which is the total volume of blood in an adult body. When the heart pumps faster, it sends out four times this amount.

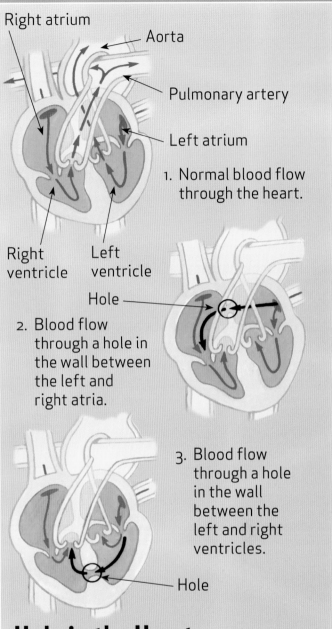

Right atrium

Aorta

Pulmonary artery

Left atrium

1. Normal blood flow through the heart.

Right ventricle

Left ventricle

Hole

2. Blood flow through a hole in the wall between the left and right atria.

3. Blood flow through a hole in the wall between the left and right ventricles.

Hole

Hole in the Heart

Some babies are born with a heart problem called "a hole in the heart." With this condition, blood from one side of the heart can mix with blood from the other side. As a result, not enough oxygen and nutrients reach the body's cells, resulting in shortness of breath, tiredness, heart failure, and even a stroke. Sometimes, these holes close naturally, but an operation may be needed.

Around and Around

The blood circulates, or flows, around the body in a system of blood vessels called the vascular network. Arteries take blood away from the heart, veins bring it back again, and tiny vessels called capillaries connect the arteries and veins.

Two Systems

Just as the heart is two pumps, the circulatory system has two parts. The arteries and veins that lead to and from the left side of the heart are known as the systemic circulation. The systemic arteries deliver oxygen, energy, nutrients, and other important substances to the body's billions of microscopic cells. The systemic veins then collect waste products.

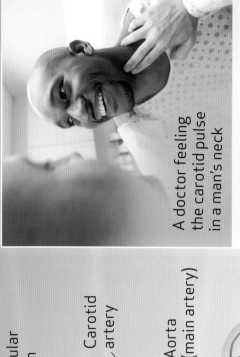

A doctor feeling the carotid pulse in a man's neck

To the Brain

Blood flows to the brain up the carotid arteries in the neck. This artery's pulse can be felt as blood surges through it with each heartbeat. In an emergency, medical staff check the carotid pulse to make sure the brain is receiving enough blood.

The main blood vessels of the circulatory system. Arteries are shown in red and veins in blue. Capillaries are too small to see in this diagram.

Jugular vein

Carotid artery

Aorta (main artery)

Superior vena cava

Heart

Lower aorta (main artery)

Inferior vena cava (main vein from body)

Iliac artery

Iliac vein

Radial artery

Lungs and Oxygen

The second set of arteries and veins takes blood from the right side of the heart to the lungs for more oxygen. This system is called the pulmonary circulation. As the blood leaves the heart, it is low in oxygen and dark reddish blue. In the lungs, the blood absorbs oxygen, turns bright red, and flows back to the left side of the heart.

Tibial vein

Tibial artery

Top Facts

- It takes a drop of blood one minute to travel around the entire systemic circulation, and less than 10 seconds to pass around the pulmonary circulation.

- In the systemic circulation, arteries carry bright red, oxygen-rich blood.

- In the pulmonary circulation, the arteries carry dark reddish blue blood that is low in oxygen.

It's Amazing!

If all your blood vessels could be taken out of your body and laid end to end, they would stretch 62,000 miles. This is the same distance as two and a half times around Earth!

After exercise, we have to stop to allow our bodies to recover.

Exhausted

During exercise, the muscles need more oxygen and energy, so the heart beats faster to supply more blood. After exercising for a while, our circulation cannot keep up. We have to slow down and breathe faster and deeper to take in more oxygen, which allows our circulation to settle down again.

Blood Cells

An adult has about 1.5 gallons of blood in his or her body. This red fluid is essential to life—without it, we would die. It does many vital jobs, including carrying oxygen around the body, removing waste, and fighting disease.

A magnified image of red blood cells

Red Blood Cells

Blood consists of billions of microscopic cells floating in a liquid called plasma. There are three main kinds of cells—the most numerous are red blood cells, also known as erythrocytes. They are shaped like doughnuts without the holes, and their main task is to take in oxygen from the lungs and release it to the organs and tissues.

It's Amazing!

A tiny drop of blood as small as a pinhead contains approximately 5 million red blood cells, 10,000 white blood cells, and 300,000 platelets.

Plasma: 55%

White blood cells and platelets: 4%

Red blood cells: 41%

What's in Blood?

More than half of blood is liquid plasma, which is mostly water. Plasma also contains nutrients, glucose, hormones, and hundreds of other substances. The red and white cells and the platelets move around in the liquid plasma.

Other Blood Cells

White blood cells, known as leukocytes, are the second kind of blood cell. These cells fight germs and disease and remove waste from the blood and body. Platelets (see pages 92-93), also called thrombocytes, are the third kind of cell. These are more like cell fragments, and their major task is to help blood clot in cuts and wounds to form a scab.

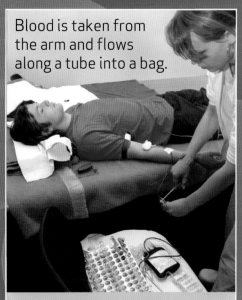

Blood is taken from the arm and flows along a tube into a bag.

Giving Blood

Many people donate, or give, blood. The body makes up the lost blood in a few days. Giving blood saves millions of lives around the world every year.

Blood Groups

In 1901, Austrian doctor Karl Landsteiner realized that not all blood is the same. Different people have blood from different groups. These groups are labeled A, B, AB, and O. If blood of the wrong group is given to a person, it can kill them.

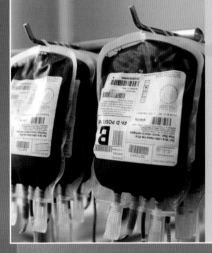

Bags of donated blood are labeled according to their blood group.

Storing Blood

Donated blood is tested for infections and to find out its blood group. It is then stored in a blood bank, ready to be used if someone needs it during an operation or after an accident. The blood is transfused, or passed, into the patient through a tube connected to a vein.

Blood Vessels

When blood leaves the heart, it passes through strong, thick-walled arteries. These split and branch many times to form tiny capillaries (see pages 90–91), which then join the veins that carry the blood back to the heart.

To the Heart

The blood flowing through the veins is under low pressure. As veins approach the heart, they get wider and wider until they pour into two very large veins. These are the superior vena cava, which brings blood from the head and arms, and the inferior vena cava, which brings blood from the legs and trunk (see pages 84–85).

Varicose Veins

Varicose veins are veins that appear as twisted lumps under the skin. They are caused by the vein walls becoming weak and the veins widening. This means that the valves cannot work properly and they allow blood to flow the wrong way. Compare this with the diagram of a properly working vein on page 81. As the blood flows the wrong way, it makes the veins bulge and forms bumps on the skin.

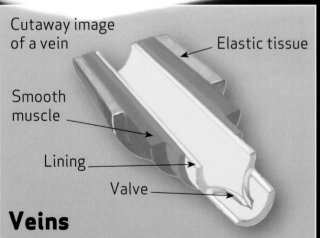

Cutaway image of a vein

Elastic tissue

Smooth muscle

Lining

Valve

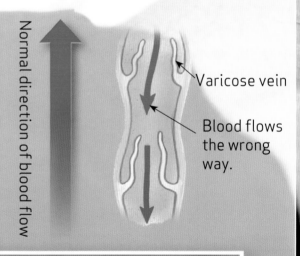

Normal direction of blood flow

Varicose vein

Blood flows the wrong way.

Veins

Small movements of the body help to propel blood through the veins toward the heart. In many of the larger veins, the inner lining has flaps that act as valves, which stop the blood from going the wrong way.

It's Amazing!

At any moment, more than 70 percent of the blood is in the veins, about 20 percent is in the arteries, and less than 10 percent is in the smallest blood vessels, the capillaries.

Looking at Blood Vessels

- Have a look at the inside of your wrist. You can probably see blue lines under the skin.

- These are veins carrying blood from the hands. You can't usually see the arteries in the wrist, because they are deeper under the skin and have thicker walls that hide the blood.

Taking blood from a vein in the arm using a hollow needle

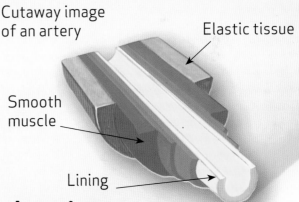

Cutaway image of an artery

Elastic tissue

Smooth muscle

Lining

Arteries

An artery's wall has several layers—the inner layer is a smooth lining along which blood flows, the middle layer is muscle, and the outer layer is elastic tissue. The muscles contract to squeeze the artery, pushing the blood along.

From the Heart

Blood is pumped from the heart under great pressure. Arteries have thicker walls than veins to withstand this high blood pressure without bursting. They also have layers of muscles in their walls that can tighten to make the artery narrower. The brain controls the width of the arteries, allowing it to alter the amount of blood that flows to each body part.

Smallest Blood Vessels

The tiniest blood vessels, the capillaries, are far too thin to see, except through a microscope. They form a fine mesh that carries important nutrients to almost every cell within your body and takes away potentially harmful waste products.

Capillary Network

Capillaries form as arteries branch again and again, becoming narrower and shorter. Almost every part of the body has a network of capillaries branching among its cells and tissues. Only a few parts, such as the lens of the eye, lack capillaries. The smallest capillaries are in the brain and intestine, and the largest are in the bone marrow and skin.

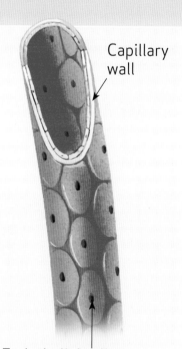

Capillary wall

Endothelial cell

Cutaway view of a capillary

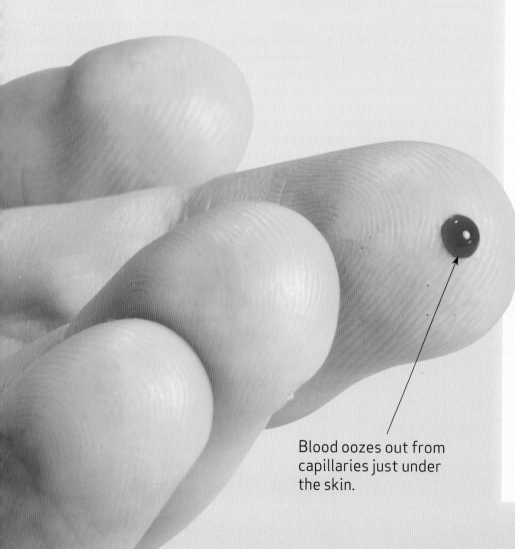

Blood oozes out from capillaries just under the skin.

Thin Walls

The wall of a capillary is made of a single layer of endothelial cells. The walls are so thin that most substances can pass through them. Red blood cells cannot pass, but white cells can squeeze through to attack germs.

Tight Squeeze

The smallest capillaries are not much wider than a red blood cell—if they were laid side by side, you could fit about 70 red blood cells across the period at the end of this sentence. The red blood cells have to line up in single file to pass through the narrowest capillaries.

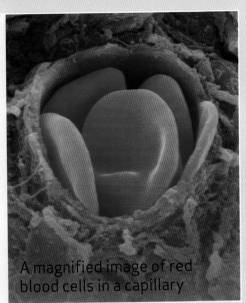

A magnified image of red blood cells in a capillary

Waste and Heat

In the lungs, oxygen passes through the network of capillaries into the blood, and the waste gas carbon dioxide goes the other way. Other waste products pass from the blood through capillaries into the kidneys and intestines, where they are removed from the body. The body also removes excess heat through the capillaries. The heat passes from the blood through capillaries into the skin, where it is released.

Top Facts

- An average capillary is 0.0004 inches wide and 0.004 inches long.

- A typical artery is about half an inch wide and 6 inches in length.

- An average vein is about half an inch wide and about 8 inches long.

- The widest artery, the aorta, measures 1 inch across.

- The largest veins, the venae cavae, are 1.2 inches across.

It's Amazing!

There are more than 10 billion capillaries running through nearly every part of the body. If they were all laid out flat, they would cover 54,000 square feet, which is almost the area of a soccer field.

Blood Pressure

Blood presses on the walls of the blood vessels as it flows through them. This force is called blood pressure and is measured using a machine called a sphygmomanometer. Two readings are usually taken—the higher systolic pressure when the heart pumps out blood, and the lower diastolic pressure when the heart relaxes.

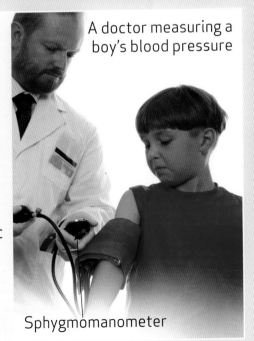

A doctor measuring a boy's blood pressure

Sphygmomanometer

Blood Clotting

One of blood's vital tasks is to seal wounds by forming a clot. If blood didn't form clots, people would bleed to death from small cuts.

Internal Clots

In addition to forming to heal a cut on the surface of the skin (see pages 18–19), blood clots form to block leaks that occur inside the body. In fact, tiny leaks are forming inside your body all the time. If your blood wasn't able to clot, then you would die from internal bleeding.

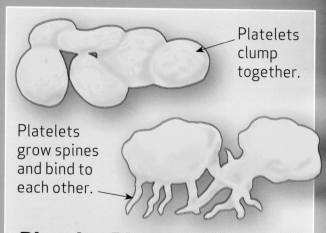

Platelets clump together.

Platelets grow spines and bind to each other.

Platelet Plugs

Within a few seconds of a blood vessel being damaged, platelets in the blood collect near the injury. They swell, become sticky, and clump together to form a plug that stops blood flowing from the wound. The plug creates a surface on which the clot can form.

Clotting Experiment

- Pour water through a sieve. It should flow through easily. Now, place a sheet of parchment paper into the sieve and slowly pour in water.

- The fibers in the paper will swell and slow the passage of water like the fibers in a blood clot.

Traveling Clots

An embolus is an object in the bloodstream that may block a blood vessel, especially where the vessel divides into smaller branches. A blood clot that forms in one part of the vessel network, such as a vein, may travel in the blood. It could block a coronary artery in the heart, causing a heart attack, or an artery in the brain, leading to a stroke.

Blood clots sometimes form in veins after surgery.

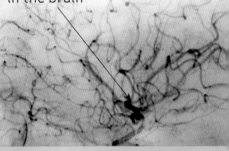

An embolism in an artery in the brain

Embolisms

Sometimes a thrombus, or clot, forms where a blood vessel is narrowed due to a build-up of fatty patches, called atheroma, in its lining. The clot may then detach to become an embolus and travel through the body.

Leeches

Leeches feed on blood, and there is a substance in their saliva that stops blood from clotting. Some surgeons use leeches today because they stop blood clotting in wounds. This keeps blood flowing to damaged body parts and speeds up recovery.

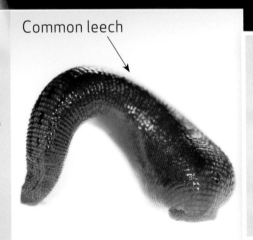

Common leech

It's Amazing!

The blood-clotting process is extremely complicated and can involve more than 30 different chemicals.

The Lymph System

A fluid called lymph travels around the body in tubes similar to blood vessels. These lymphatics, or lymph vessels, have small masses of tissue along them called lymph nodes.

Lymph Fluid

Lymph is a pale, clear fluid that collects between cells and tissues. It flows into lymph vessels and ends up in larger vessels called lymphatic ducts. These empty the lymph into the blood system.

One-Way Flow

Unlike the circulatory system, the lymph system does not flow in a cycle. Instead, it starts with tiny, dead-end capillaries, which form a network of tubes that weave between tissue cells. The walls of the capillaries are just one cell thick. Fluid from the tissue moves into the capillaries through openings between the cells in the lymph capillary wall.

Tissue cell

Endothelial cell (lymph capillary lining)

Lymph

Opening in capillary

Fluid from tissue enters lymph

Ending of lymph capillary

Tonsils

Cervical (neck) nodes

Thymus gland

Spleen

Lumbar nodes

Inguinal nodes

Iliac nodes

Thoracic duct

Intestinal nodes

What Lymph Does

Like blood, lymph delivers nutrients and takes away waste. It also carries white blood cells that fight germs and disease (see pages 96–97). The lymph nodes are packed with white blood cells, which clean the lymph and kill germs. There is no pump like the heart to push lymph around the body. Instead, it flows slowly, squeezed by muscles around the lymph vessels. Lymph only moves when the body's muscles are active.

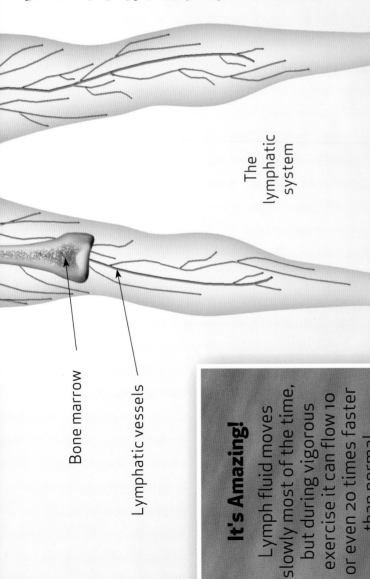

The lymphatic system

Bone marrow

Lymphatic vessels

Top Facts

- The average adult body contains between 1 and 2 quarts of lymph fluid.
- Each lymph node is 0.04 and 1 inch wide.
- Nodes get their name from a Latin word that means "knot," because the rows of nodes resemble knots in a piece of string.

It's Amazing!

Lymph fluid moves slowly most of the time, but during vigorous exercise it can flow 10 or even 20 times faster than normal.

White Cells

Billions of white blood cells patrol the body through the lymph system and the blood. These white blood cells are produced in the bone marrow inside the larger bones. During illness, their numbers can increase more than 10 times as they work to combat germs.

White blood cell

Fighting Disease

If a germ enters your body, it can make you unwell. Your body has a mini army of different white blood cells, such as lymphocytes, neutrophils, and macrophages, and organs, such as the spleen, that are always ready to fight germs. These make up your body's immune system.

A magnified image of a macrophage attacking bacteria

First Line of Attack

Any germs that enter the body are attacked by white blood cells called macrophages. Each macrophage surrounds a germ and carries it in the lymph to a lymph node. There, other white blood cells called lymphocytes get to work.

White Globules

White blood cells were first identified through a microscope in the 18th century. The role of these white cells was not understood at the time, and they were called "white globules of pus."

Vessel brings lymph to node

Blood vessels

Vessel draining lymph from node

Cutaway view of a lymph node

Lymph nodule

Lymph Nodes

White blood cells called lymphocytes multiply and are stored inside the lymph nodes. Lymph flows into the node, bringing germs and other harmful substances to these concentrations of white blood cells.

Germ Destroyers

Macrophages can destroy things that the body doesn't recognize as belonging to it, including bacteria. They can surround the invader and digest it in a process that is called phagocytosis.

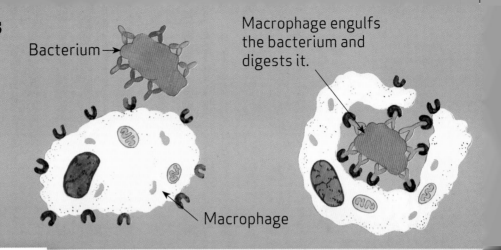

Bacterium →

Macrophage engulfs the bacterium and digests it.

Macrophage

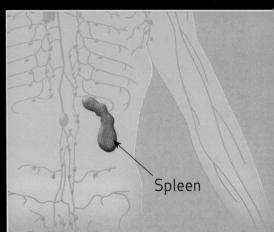

Spleen

Spleen

The spleen is an organ that filters waste substances from the blood and lymph. It also acts as a large store for red and white blood cells, in case the body loses a lot of blood suddenly.

Lymphocytes

Lymphocytes identify germs by recognizing foreign substances on their surfaces, called antigens. Lymphocytes then produce substances called antibodies that find other germs of this type and stick to them. Macrophages then destroy the germs and antibodies. Some antibodies remain in the body, so that it

Heart and Blood Problems

The heart and blood play such a vital role in keeping the body alive that any problems with them can be serious. If a problem is found, however, there are many modern treatments that can help.

A doctor listens to a boy's heart through a stethoscope.

Fainting

Sometimes, the heart cannot pump enough blood up to the brain. This may happen if a person has to stand for a long time, especially in hot weather. The body's reaction is to faint—lose consciousness and fall over. Fainting brings the heart level with the head, so it can pump blood to the brain more easily.

Hearing the Heart

Doctors listen to the sounds of a heartbeat to make sure the heart is working properly. Unusual sounds, known as murmurs, may indicate that the blood is not flowing normally.

Standing for a long time has made this soldier faint.

Heart Attack

A heart attack happens when the blood flow to the heart is interrupted, which may be because of a blood clot (see pages 92–93) blocking an artery. Without oxygen or energy, the heart muscle cannot beat properly. This causes chest pain, breathlessness, sweating, and feeling of faintness. If the blood flow to the heart is not restored within about 40 minutes, the heart muscle will begin to die.

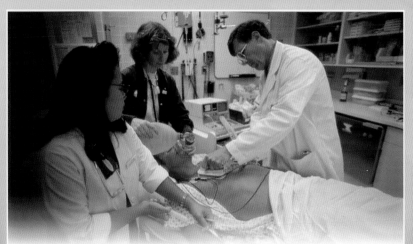

Medical staff use a defibrillator in an emergency.

Shocking the Heart

A heart that is not beating properly can be shocked into a regular rhythm using an electrical charge. This is passed into the heart via two pads on the chest from a machine called a defibrillator.

Bad Blood

Until the end of the 19th century, many doctors treated a wide variety of illnesses by blood-letting. This involved cutting a patient, in the belief that removing the "bad blood" would stop an illness from getting worse.

It's Amazing!

With modern emergency treatments, such as defibrillators, the chances of surviving a heart attack are twice what they were 50 years ago.

Too Narrow

Over many years, a diet that is too high in fats (see pages 106–107) can lead to a fatty substance building up in the lining of the arteries. This condition, called atherosclerosis, makes the arteries narrow and harden, decreasing the flow of blood and making it more likely that a clot will form.

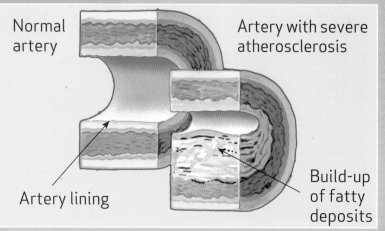

Normal artery

Artery with severe atherosclerosis

Artery lining

Build-up of fatty deposits

Healthy Heart and Blood

All muscles need exercise or they will become weak and waste away. The heart is almost all muscle and, like all muscles, it gets stronger if it is exercised on a regular basis.

Daily Exercise

Exercise keeps the lungs, bones, joints, and many other body parts healthy, but it doesn't have to involve playing sports or working out in the gym. Exercise can be a part of daily life, such as walking or cycling rather than sitting in a car, or using the stairs rather than elevators or escalators.

It's Amazing!

An average person's heart pumps more than 100,000 times a day and 40 million times a year. Over a lifetime, this adds up to around three billion beats.

Playing a sport, such as soccer, is a great way to get the heart pumping fast.

Top Facts

To keep your circulatory system healthy, you should:

- Exercise regularly—at least two or three times a week for at least 20 minutes.

- Eat a balanced diet, low in fats, salt, and processed foods.

- Keep your weight at a healthy level.

- Not smoke.

- Try to reduce worry, stress, and anxiety.

Quit It!

Aside from damaging the lungs, smoking makes it more likely that blood vessels will narrow. It also reduces the ability of the blood to carry oxygen.

Smoking increases the risk of heart disease.

Importance of Diet

What we eat also has a great effect on the heart and blood. Eating foods that contain a lot of the mineral iron (see below) helps to keep our red blood cells healthy. On the other hand, eating too much salt can cause blood pressure to rise and put extra strain on the heart and blood vessels.

Eat Well

Eating a balanced diet helps to keep the digestive system working well and contains all the vitamins and minerals needed to keep the blood healthy.

A salad containing a lot of vegetables is a healthy choice for a meal.

Iron-rich food	Iron content per 100 g	RDA %
Cockles, boiled	28 mg	155%
Liver	9 mg	50%
Fish paste	9 mg	50%
Kidney	8 mg	44%
Venison	7.8 mg	43%
Mussels, boiled	7 mg	39%
Liver pâté	7 mg	39%
Liver sausage	6.4 mg	36%
Goose	5 mg	28%
Shrimps	5 mg	28%
Sardines	4.5 mg	27%
Anchovies	4 mg	22%
Whitebait	4 mg	22%
Lean beef	2.5 mg	16%

A list of foods with high levels of iron. The RDA—recommended daily allowance—is the amount of a nutrient that experts recommend a person should eat each day.

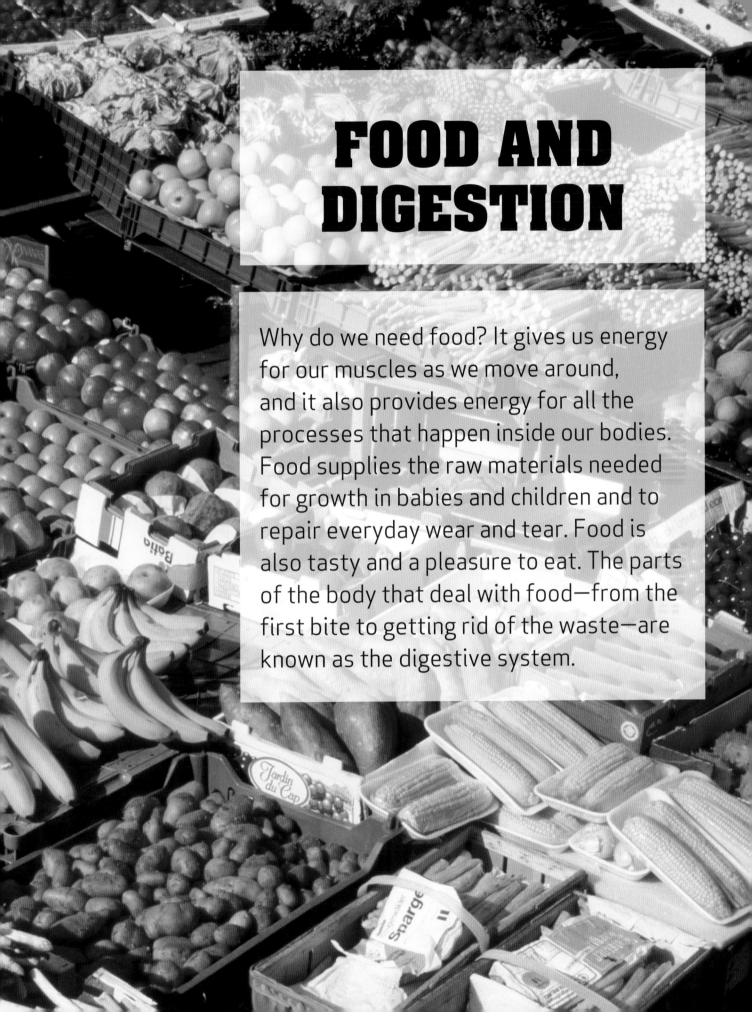

FOOD AND DIGESTION

Why do we need food? It gives us energy for our muscles as we move around, and it also provides energy for all the processes that happen inside our bodies. Food supplies the raw materials needed for growth in babies and children and to repair everyday wear and tear. Food is also tasty and a pleasure to eat. The parts of the body that deal with food—from the first bite to getting rid of the waste—are known as the digestive system.

Food's Journey

Swallowing is the start of a long journey for your food that takes 24 hours or more and involves traveling up to 30 feet through a dark tube full of powerful chemicals.

Digestive Tract

The digestive tract is a long tube that starts at the mouth and ends at the anus. Food is chewed in the mouth, swallowed down the throat, and pushed through the esophagus, or gullet, into the stomach. It then travels through the small and large intestines to the anus, where any waste is passed out.

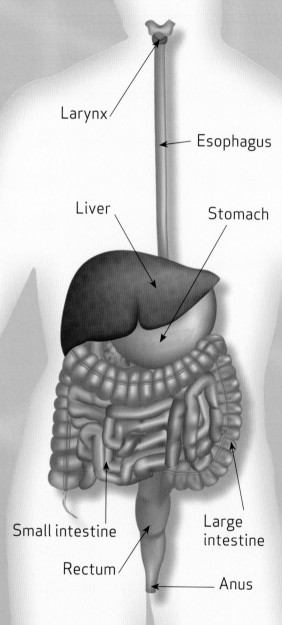

Larynx

Esophagus

Liver

Stomach

Small intestine

Large intestine

Rectum

Anus

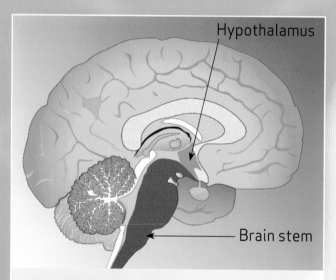

Hypothalamus

Brain stem

Thinking of Food

The brain plays a vital role in digestion. A part called the hypothalamus makes us feel hungry and thirsty. The brain stem lies between the spinal cord and the upper brain. It controls the automatic movements of the gut and the removal of food waste.

Food Study

In 1822, American doctor William Beaumont treated a patient who had been shot in the stomach. The small bullet hole was kept open and provided a "window" for studying what happened in the stomach. Beaumont poked into the hole and took samples of the chemicals that the stomach made after the patient ate.

Most of the digestive system is packed into the lower half of the body—the abdomen.

Breaking Down Food

In the digestive tract, food is digested, or broken down, and absorbed into the body. Anything that isn't absorbed or used by the body is expelled as waste. Several other body parts help with the digestion of food, including the liver and pancreas. They create some of the chemicals needed to break down and absorb food.

Plenty of Water

In addition to food, the body needs water. Water is essential for almost every process in the body—from digestion to sweating. Some water is contained in food, but everyone should also drink plenty of water.

The body needs water to survive.

Big Eater

Elephants have huge bodies, which need a lot of energy. They eat mainly grass, leaves, and other plant foods that are low in nourishment. So, to get enough energy from its diet, an adult elephant must eat for about 18 to 20 hours every day. An elephant can eat more than 440 pounds of plant food daily, which is about the weight of three adult humans.

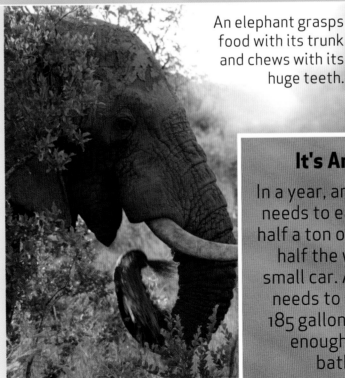

An elephant grasps food with its trunk and chews with its huge teeth.

It's Amazing!

In a year, an adult human needs to eat more than half a ton of food. That's half the weight of a small car. An adult also needs to drink about 185 gallons of water— enough to fill 50 bathtubs.

What's in Food?

Food is not just needed to fill us up and ward off hunger. It also contains hundreds of substances that your body must have to stay fit and healthy and to work well.

This food pyramid shows how much of each type of food you should eat in a healthy diet.

Fats

Sugar

The Right Balance

The body needs the right balance of different types of food. Too much of any single food item can cause harm. A healthy balance contains plenty of fruit and vegetables; grains, such as bread, pasta, and rice; some fish, dairy produce, nuts, pulses, or a small amount of meat. Foods that are high in sugar and fat should only be eaten in small quantities.

Dairy, meat, fish, eggs, pulses, and nuts

Fruit and vegetables

It's Amazing!

Every few weeks, a new fad diet comes and goes. But the basics of healthy eating have been the same since people lived in caves!

Grains: bread, pasta, rice, and cereal

Food for Energy

Different foods contain a variety of substances, and they all perform different roles once they have been absorbed by the body. For example, vitamins and minerals help to keep the body working well. Proteins are important for building new cells and tissue, as well as repairing damaged ones. Carbohydrates are used to supply the energy we need to live.

Fresh fruit contains a lot of vitamins and minerals.

Vitamins and Minerals

There are many vitamins and minerals that are important to your body. For example, vitamin C helps to keep your gums healthy, while vitamin D helps to keep your bones strong. The mineral iron is important for healthy blood.

Top Facts

- An important part of food, which the body does not digest, is fiber. Fiber helps the intestines to stay healthy. Fruit and vegetables and wholemeal foods—in which every part of the grain is used—contain a lot of fiber.

- Processed foods have been changed so much that they lose some of their natural goodness. White bread, for example, has very little fiber left.

Protein

Meat, fish, eggs, nuts, pulses, and cheese contain a lot of protein. Your body breaks down the protein you eat into simpler chemicals called amino acids. It can then use these amino acids to build new proteins to make and repair body cells.

Meat and fish contain a lot of protein.

Carbohydrates

Cakes and bread are foods that contain a lot of carbohydrates. While your body needs these substances to make energy, if you eat too many carbohydrates, your body turns them into fat. It then stores this fat in a layer just under the skin called adipose tissue.

Bread contains a lot of carbohydrates.

Teeth and Biting

Teeth bite, grind, and chew food to make it easier to swallow and digest. They are coated with enamel—the hardest material in the body—so that they last a long time. In fact, you will only have two sets of teeth throughout your entire lifetime!

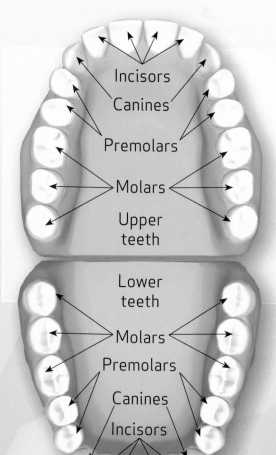

Incisors
Canines
Premolars
Molars
Upper teeth

Lower teeth
Molars
Premolars
Canines
Incisors

The Full Set

An adult has 32 teeth. There are four different types of teeth—8 incisors at the front, 4 canines next to them, 8 premolars, and then 12 molars at the rear of the mouth.

Eating an apple would be difficult without teeth.

Baby Teeth

How many teeth you have depends partly on your age. Babies have no teeth or very few. Then, small "baby," or milk, teeth appear, with most children having a full set of 20 baby teeth by about the age of three or four. From about six or seven years old, these teeth start to fall out and are replaced by adult ones.

Look at Your Tooth Prints

- Choose a crunchy fruit, such as an apple, and bite into it with your front teeth to take out a chunk.
- Look at the tooth prints in the area you have bitten. Can you see the separate tooth marks and the curve of the teeth in your jaws?
- Ask some friends to do the same and compare your tooth prints.

Uses of Teeth

Teeth are like tools and have different shapes for different tasks. The chisel-like incisors at the front have straight, narrow edges for biting and slicing food. The canines, or eyeteeth, next to the incisors are tall and pointed to tear and rip. The premolars and molars, or cheek teeth, are broad and flat with rounded bumps for crushing and chewing.

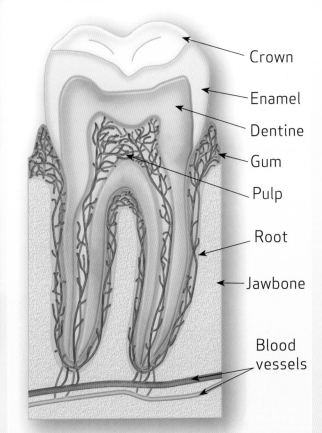

Crown
Enamel
Dentine
Gum
Pulp
Root
Jawbone
Blood vessels

Inside a Tooth

A tooth has two parts—the crown above the gum and the roots below. The top layer of the crown is made of enamel. Beneath this is dentine, which is also a very tough material, and in the middle is the soft pulp. Blood vessels supply the tooth with nutrients.

It's Amazing!

The four molars right at the back of the mouth are the last teeth to appear, at about 17 to 20 years of age. Because they grow in adulthood, they are known as wisdom teeth. In some people, they never appear—perhaps because there is not enough room.

Hunting Teeth

Lions and other hunting animals have very large, pointed canine teeth for stabbing into prey and ripping flesh. Lions also have sharp-edged molar teeth called carnassials for cutting into tough meat.

Canines
Carnassials

Chewing and Swallowing

After you have taken a bite using the sharp incisor teeth at the front of your mouth (see pages 108–109), your tongue pushes the food around so that it can reach the molar teeth at the back. These crush the food up so that it makes a pulp, which is easier to swallow.

A Mushy Mess

A liquid called saliva, or spit, helps moisten and soften the food and make it even more squishy. Saliva is made in six glands on the sides of the face, which release up to 1.5 quarts a day into the mouth. There is a regular slow release of saliva to keep the mouth and lips moist, but during eating much more saliva flows.

This young girl is learning how to eat, by coordinating the movements of her lips, tongue, and jaws. It can be a messy business!

Salivary Glands

There are three salivary glands located on each side of the face. The parotid gland is just in front of the ear. The submandibular gland is at the back of the lower jaw. The sublingual gland is under the tongue.

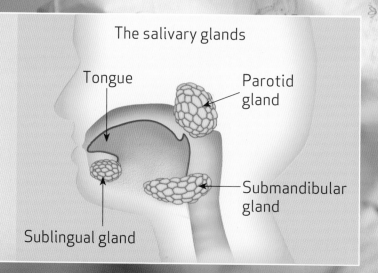

The salivary glands

Tongue

Parotid gland

Submandibular gland

Sublingual gland

Study a Swallow

- Stand in front of a mirror and watch and feel your neck carefully.

- Get ready to swallow and feel how your neck muscles tighten.

- As you swallow, see and feel how your upper neck bulges.

- Feel your lower neck as the movement passes downward and the swallow ends.

Chemical Attack

Saliva contains a substance called an enzyme. Enzymes attack food and break it down into more simple chemicals. The enzyme in saliva is known as amylase. It breaks apart starchy substances in food. This is the first of many chemical processes that play a part in digestion.

It's Amazing!

An average person bites and chews food more than 1,000 times each day. This helps to keep the jaw muscles strong and healthy.

1. Food is pushed to back of mouth.

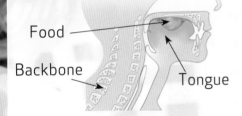

Food

Backbone

Tongue

2. Food reaches upper throat.

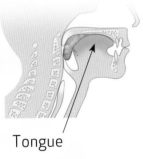

Tongue

Swallowing

(1) At the start of swallowing, the tongue separates part of the mouthful of food and pushes it to the back of the mouth. (2) The back of the tongue forces the food down into the upper throat. (3) The lower throat tightens, and a flap—the epiglottis—folds down over the entrance to the trachea. (4) Muscles in the esophagus "grab" the food as it passes over the epiglottis. (5) The food begins its journey down the esophagus.

3. Epiglottis covers trachea.

4. Food enters esophagus.

5. Food is swallowed.

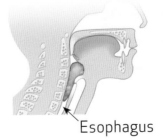

Trachea

Epiglottis

Esophagus

Epiglottis

In the Stomach

Swallowed food takes a few seconds to travel down the esophagus. It is pushed into the baglike stomach, which attacks the food with powerful acids, enzymes, and other chemicals.

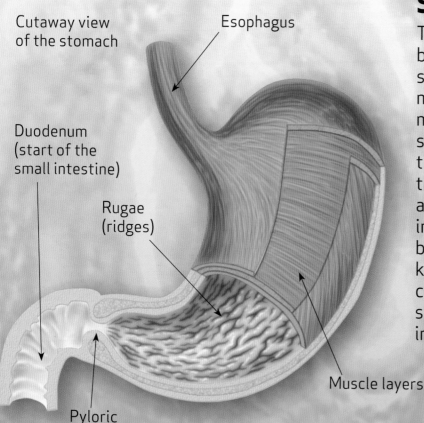

Cutaway view of the stomach

Esophagus

Duodenum (start of the small intestine)

Rugae (ridges)

Muscle layers

Pyloric sphincter

Stomach

The stomach is a bag that sits just below the left lung. Its walls have several layers—three of these are made of muscle fibers. The muscles tighten and contract the stomach to squash, mix, and mash the food inside. The entrance to the stomach from the esophagus and the exit into the part of the intestine called the duodenum both have rings of muscle fibers known as sphincters. These stay closed to keep the food in the stomach until it is ready to pass into the intestines.

Stomach Wall

The inside of the stomach wall is folded into ridges called rugae, which allow the stomach to stretch. The innermost layer of the stomach wall is the mucosa. The next layer is the tough and stretchy submucosa. The three muscle layers are next, forming the outside of the stomach.

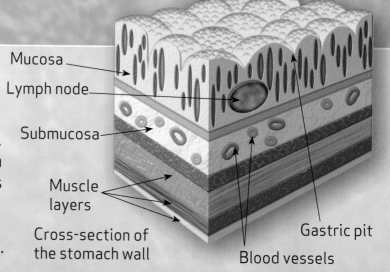

Mucosa

Lymph node

Submucosa

Muscle layers

Cross-section of the stomach wall

Gastric pit

Blood vessels

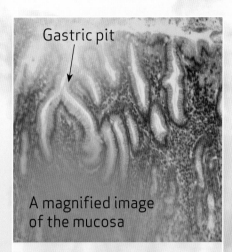

Gastric pit

A magnified image
of the mucosa

Warning! Acid!

Hydrochloric acid is
an extremely strong
chemical. It is more
than 10 times more
powerful than the
acidic juices found
in vinegar and lemon.

Gastric Pits

The mucosa has thousands
of gastric pits. These are
lined with cells that
make a wide range of
chemicals, including slimy
mucus, hydrochloric acid,
and the enzyme pepsin.

Stomach Juices

Apart from mashing the food physically, the stomach
attacks the food with powerful chemicals. Its
lining produces a strong acid called hydrochloric acid.
The lining also makes more of the chemicals called
enzymes. These get to work breaking down different
parts of the meal. For example, lipase attacks fatty
foods and pepsin breaks down proteins.

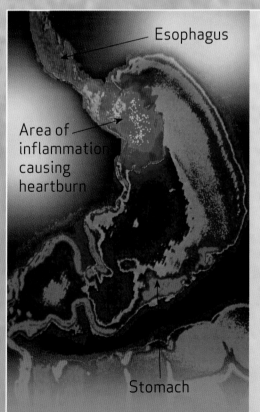

Esophagus

Area of
inflammation
causing
heartburn

Stomach

Heartburn

In some people, the
contents of the stomach
seep back up into the
esophagus, or lower
gullet. This causes
inflammation and pain
in the chest, where the
acid attacks the gullet
lining. The pain is known
as heartburn, although it
has nothing to do with
the heart.

An image showing
inflammation caused
by stomach contents
entering the esophagus

Top Facts

• Your stomach
  begins to contract
  and produce juices
  as soon as you see
  or smell food.

• An adult stomach
  can hold up to
  1 quart of food
  and drink.

• Most food stays in
  the stomach for one
  to four hours.

• Fatty foods stay
  in the stomach
  for longer.

Guts Galore

After a few hours in the stomach, even the most beautiful-looking meal has become a thick, dark, mushy "soup." There is more digestion to come, however, in the next part of the digestive tract—the small intestine.

Gut Pioneer

In 1780, Italian scientist Lazzaro Spallanzani wrote a book about digestion. He did many experiments on his own digestive system, such as swallowing food in net bags on long pieces of string and pulling them back up to see what had happened.

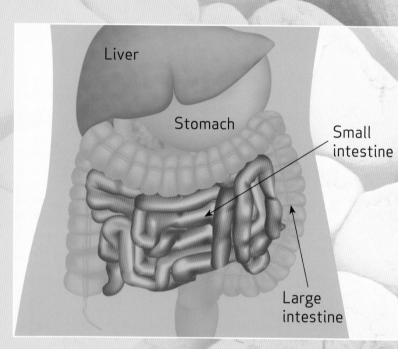

Liver

Stomach

Small intestine

Large intestine

Small Intestine

The small intestine, or small bowel, is a narrow but very long tube. It has three parts—first, the duodenum, which is the shortest section; then the middle section, the jejunum; and finally the longest section, the ileum, which connects to the large intestine. The small intestine is coiled, looped, and folded into the middle of the lower body and is almost surrounded by the next part of the digestive tract, the large intestine.

More Digestion

The small intestine contains many more enzymes that attack food and continue breaking it into smaller pieces. Most of these enzymes are not made in the small intestine but come from another digestive organ called the pancreas, which is found in the left side of the body under the stomach.

A microscopic image of the villi in the lining of the small intestine

Intestine Lining

The small intestine has many folds in its lining. The folds are made of millions of tiny fingerlike parts called villi. Each single villus has a system of tiny vessels inside—some are for blood, but a larger one, the lacteal, is for the fluid known as lymph (see pages 94–95). Nutrients pass into the blood and the lymph. The folds and villi give a huge surface area for absorbing nutrients.

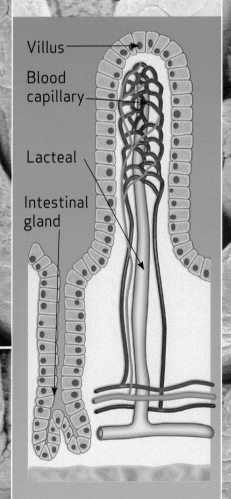

Villus

Blood capillary

Lacteal

Intestinal gland

Taking In

As food reaches its last stages of digestion, the small intestine has another job—it soaks up, or absorbs, the resulting nutrients. These nutrients are small enough to seep through the lining of the small intestine into the blood, which carries them away to the liver.

It's Amazing!

At about 20 feet, the small intestine is the longest part of the digestive tract. If it were straight rather than bent, a person would need to be almost 26 feet tall!

Breaking Down Food

The diagram on the right shows approximately how long food spends in each part of the digestive tract. During the food's travels through the guts, different enzymes break down different types of food. For example, only carbohydrates are broken down in the mouth. Both carbohydrates and proteins are broken down in the stomach, while fats are mainly broken down in the small intestine.

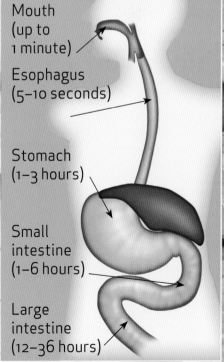

Mouth (up to 1 minute)

Esophagus (5–10 seconds)

Stomach (1–3 hours)

Small intestine (1–6 hours)

Large intestine (12–36 hours)

On the Way Out

After digestion and absorption in the small intestine, the next part of the digestive tract is the large intestine. Its main tasks are to take a few more nutrients from the remaining digested food and to remove as much water as the body needs. The waste matter is then ready for removal.

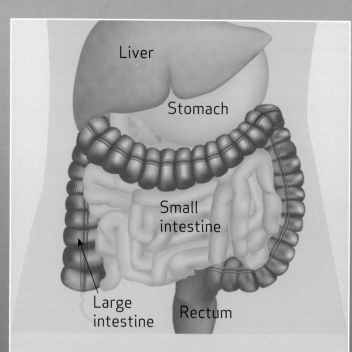

Tiny Helpers

The large intestine contains millions of tiny helpers—minute living things of various kinds, mainly bacteria. These microbes are "friendly" and work with the body. They can digest some things that the body cannot, such as certain plant foods. The microbes use some of these digested products, while the body absorbs the rest. The gut provides the microbes with a safe, warm, moist, food-filled place to live.

Large Intestine

At about 5 feet long, the large intestine is much shorter than the small intestine, but it is wider—about 2 inches wide. It forms a type of frame around the abdomen with the small intestine inside it. The large intestine is sometimes called the colon. Its strong muscles push the partly digested food along by contracting and relaxing, creating pulses of movement. The large intestine lining is coated in mucus that lubricates the inside and helps the food move smoothly.

Top Facts

- In an average person, more than half of the feces, or solid waste, is water. Much of the rest is undigested food material, such as fiber.

- The brown color of feces is due to a substance called bilirubin that comes from the breakdown of old red blood cells in the liver.

An X-ray showing a barium meal

Barium

Inside the Large Intestine

This X-ray picture was taken after a substance called barium was put into the gut. The barium shows up white on X-rays and helps to reveal the colon.

The Final Stage

The last part of the large intestine is a short wide tube called the rectum. The feces collects there before it is finally squeezed out through the anus. This double ring of muscles loosens to allow the feces to leave during the emptying of the bowels, known as defecation.

Treating Waste

From the toilet, bodily waste goes through the sewage system to a waste treatment plant. The waste is smelly and can cause disease, so it is treated at the plant to make it harmless.

Tanks of waste at a waste treatment plant

Young children have no control over going to the toilet, but it is something they learn as they grow up.

Liver and Pancreas

The liver and the pancreas are both part of the digestive system although they are not in the digestive tract. The liver is in the upper right abdomen, and the pancreas is to its left, below and behind the stomach.

Right lobe

Ligament

Left lobe

The liver is wedge-shaped and dark red, with a large right lobe and a smaller left one separated by a ligament.

Gallbladder

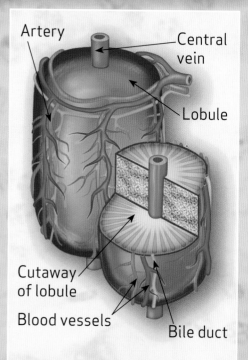

Artery

Central vein

Lobule

Cutaway of lobule

Blood vessels

Bile duct

The Liver

The liver has many jobs. One is to make bile, a green fluid that passes to a small storage bag called the gallbladder. When food enters the small intestine, bile flows in and helps to break up fat in the meal. After food is digested and absorbed, nutrients are carried in the blood to the liver, where they are stored, broken down further, or sent around the body in the blood.

Liver Lobules

The liver has thousands of tiny units, or lobules, that are made up of a central vein surrounded by groups of liver cells. These take in nutrients, make poisons harmless, and produce bile.

The Pancreas

The pancreas makes digestive juices that flow through a duct into the small intestine. These juices help neutralize the stomach acid so it doesn't burn the gut. They also contain enzymes that help to break down protein, starch, and fat in food so that they can be absorbed.

A very magnified image of the islets of Langerhans in the pancreas

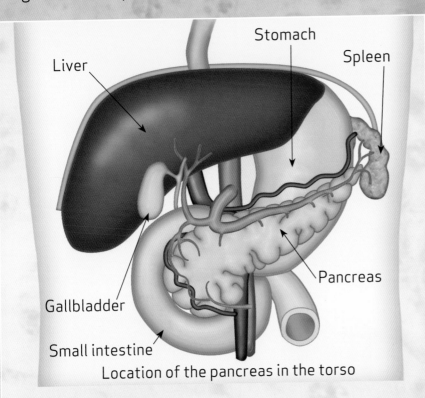

Liver

Stomach

Spleen

Pancreas

Gallbladder

Small intestine

Location of the pancreas in the torso

Hormone Maker

The pale pink pancreas is about 8 inches long and lies alongside the stomach, with the small intestine looping around it. The pancreas contains about one million tiny groups of cells known as islets of Langerhans. These produce messenger chemicals called hormones, two of which are insulin and glucagon, which help to control the blood's level of the sugar glucose. Blood glucose is the body's main source of energy. Surrounding the islets are cell groups called acini, which make the digestive juices.

Pancreas Test

One of the first scientists to study the pancreas carefully was Regnier de Graaf of the Netherlands. In 1664 he produced a report on his experiments, which were carried out mainly on dogs. He collected and tested pancreatic juices, saliva, and bile from the dogs.

People with diabetes check their blood glucose level using a special machine.

Sugar Levels

Diabetes is an illness in which the body cannot control its blood glucose level. It is caused by the lack of a hormone called insulin, or cells being unable to react properly to it.

Filtering Blood

Liquid waste, also known as urine, comes from the kidneys, which filter unwanted substances from the blood. The urine is excreted, or released, by the body from the bladder.

Waste Removal

In addition to delivering nutrients around the body, the blood collects waste and unwanted products from cells and tissue. These waste products are then removed from the blood by the urinary system and excreted as a liquid called urine.

Filtering Test

- Stir some salt and ground pepper in a small cup of water.

- Pour the water through a paper towel into another cup. See how the paper traps the larger pepper particles.

- Leave the filtered water to dry up. The salt crystals should be left behind at the bottom. Like the paper, the kidneys filter out some substances, but let others remain.

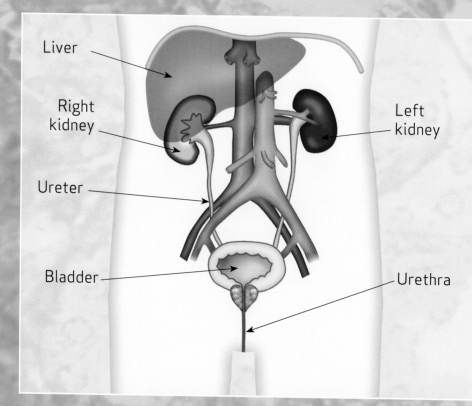

Liver

Right kidney

Ureter

Bladder

Left kidney

Urethra

The Urinary System

The urinary system consists of two kidneys at the back of the upper abdomen. From these, two tubes called ureters carry urine down to the bladder—a stretchy bag that holds the urine until it is excreted out of the body. The urine then passes down another tube called the urethra on its way out of the bladder and out of the body.

The urinary system

Nephrons

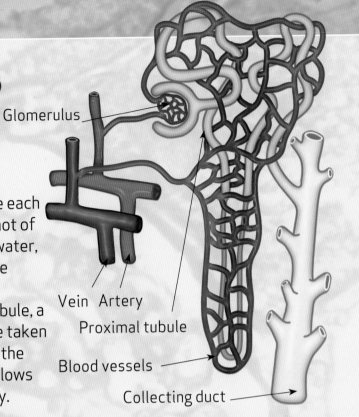

Cutaway of kidney showing nephron

In each kidney, there are about a million microscopic filters called nephrons. Inside each nephron, blood flows through a tangled knot of capillaries called the glomerulus. Waste, water, and some useful substances ooze from the glomerulus into a narrow tube called the proximal tubule. As they flow along the tubule, a lot of the water and useful substances are taken back into the blood in tiny vessels around the tubule. The leftover liquid is urine, which flows into a collecting duct and out of the kidney.

Glomerulus

Vein Artery

Proximal tubule

Blood vessels

Collecting duct

A magnified image of a glomerulus

Micturition

All of the body's blood passes through and is filtered by the kidneys every 10 minutes. This means that your blood is filtered about 150 times a day. Once filtered, the urine passes into the bladder. Your bladder can hold about half a quart of urine, although it is stretchy enough to hold twice that amount. However, when there is about 0.2 quarts of urine in the bladder, you will feel the need to micturate, or go to the bathroom.

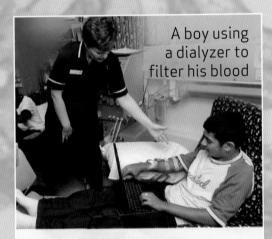

A boy using a dialyzer to filter his blood

Kidney Problems

When kidneys become diseased or fail, the blood cannot be filtered properly and waste builds up. A kidney dialysis machine must be used to do the kidneys' job for them. Blood flows along a tube into the machine, where the blood is filtered and waste is removed.

Waste and Water

The body is made mostly of water. Some of this water is used to remove waste from the blood, some is lost in sweat, and some is breathed out of the lungs as water vapor (see pages 76–77).

Replacing Water

Most of the water lost by the body is replaced by water coming in as food and drink. Some food, including many fruits and vegetables, contain about 90 percent water. Most people need to take in nearly 3 quarts of water a day, but if the weather is hot or if people lead an active lifestyle—which will increase sweating—they will need to take in a lot more. If they do not take in enough water, they may become dehydrated.

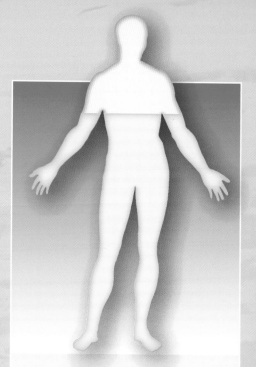

Water Levels

The body is between 61 and 64 percent water. This proportion is higher in children and lower in older people. It varies throughout the day, depending on how much you have eaten or drunk and how hot it is.

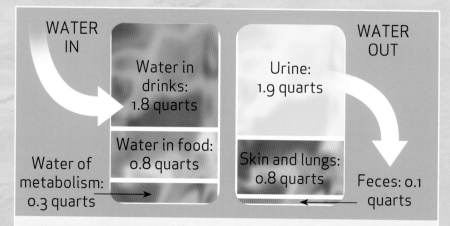

WATER IN

Water in drinks: 1.8 quarts

Water in food: 0.8 quarts

Water of metabolism: 0.3 quarts

WATER OUT

Urine: 1.9 quarts

Skin and lungs: 0.8 quarts

Feces: 0.1 quarts

Water Balance

In a day, your body gains about 3 quarts of water. Not only does this come from food and drink, but your body also makes water during its chemical activities (see right). Your body also loses about 3 quarts of water every day.

Top Facts

- Fresh urine does not have much odor, but old urine smells of ammonia. This is a gas that is released when bacteria start to break down the urine.

- Urine is mostly water, but it also contains some salts and a chemical called urea.

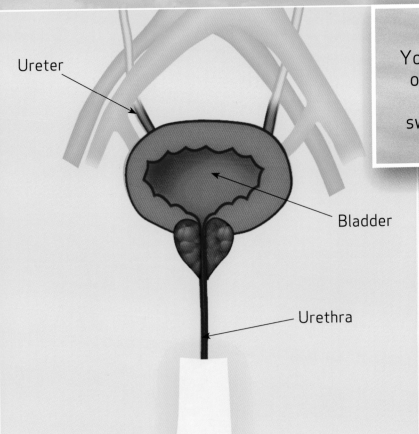

Ureter

Bladder

Urethra

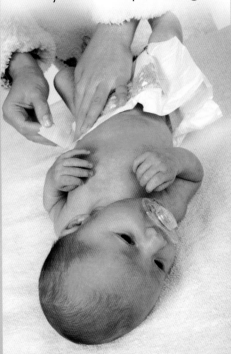

A baby has its diaper changed.

The Bladder

When the bladder is empty, it is shrunken and wrinkled. As it fills with urine, its stretchy walls expand and become smoother. Urine trickles into the bladder slowly through the two ureters. To pass urine, or urinate, the ring of muscle around the exit to the bladder relaxes. At the same time, the muscle fibers in the bladder wall tighten to squeeze out the urine.

Urinating

As the bladder fills, stretch sensors in its wall warn us that it is time to go to the bathroom. Just as babies need to learn how to defecate (see page 117), they also need to learn how to control the muscles in their bladder and urethra. Until then, they have to wear a diaper.

Making Water

One of the ways your body produces water is by releasing energy from nutrients in the blood, such as glucose. The word for all the chemical processes in the body is *metabolism*, and water made in this way is called "water of metabolism."

Digestive Problems

Names like "stomachache" and "indigestion" are given to all kinds of abdominal discomfort and pains. These pains are often caused by trapped gas, or bloating, from digestion. Conditions such as infections or ulcers are less common and more serious.

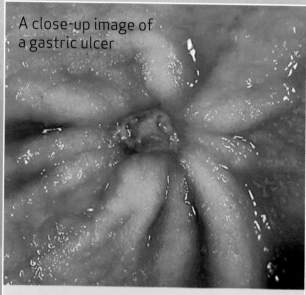

A close-up image of a gastric ulcer

Bowel Changes

Diarrhea occurs when the feces are watery and runny. It can make the body lose too much water and lead to dehydration. Constipation is when the feces are hard and dry and may get stuck in the intestine. There are many causes of these conditions, from eating contaminated food to stress or shock.

Peptic Ulcers

A peptic ulcer is a raw, exposed patch of the digestive lining. In the stomach, it is called a gastric ulcer. In the first part of the small intestine, it is called a duodenal ulcer. Most people with peptic ulcers have particular bacteria—*Helicobacter pylori*—in their gut. Peptic ulcers can also be caused by smoking and excessive use of certain drugs, such as aspirin.

Ulcer Breakthrough

In 1982, medical scientists John Robin Warren and Barry Marshall discovered a bacterium that may be the cause of peptic ulcers. Before their work, many people thought that ulcers were probably caused by consuming too much spicy food, alcohol, and caffeine.

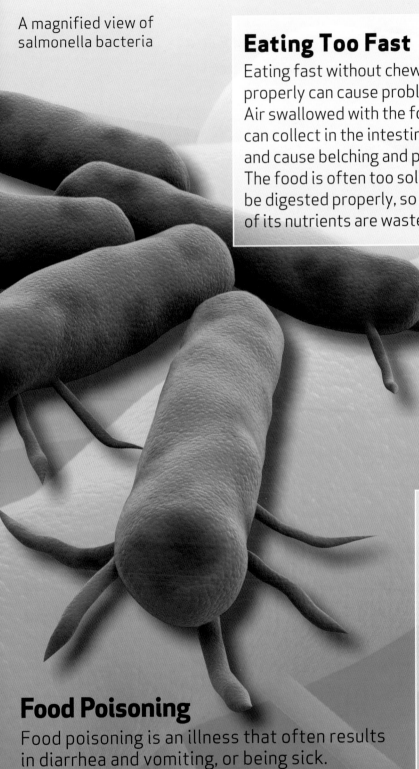

A magnified view of salmonella bacteria

Eating Too Fast

Eating fast without chewing properly can cause problems. Air swallowed with the food can collect in the intestines and cause belching and pain. The food is often too solid to be digested properly, so many of its nutrients are wasted.

It's Amazing!

In the United States, there are around 76 million cases of food-borne illness every single year!

The Appendix

The appendix is a small closed tube that sticks out from the first part of the large intestine. It has no role in the digestion process. However, it can become blocked and infected, in which case it will have to be removed.

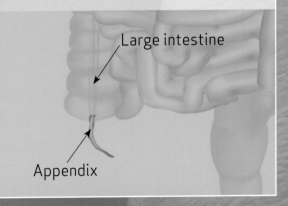

Large intestine

Appendix

Food Poisoning

Food poisoning is an illness that often results in diarrhea and vomiting, or being sick. It can be caused by germs, such as the bacteria salmonella, entering the body from infected food. Some foods, such as certain types of mushrooms, contain powerful chemicals that can be poisonous or harmful.

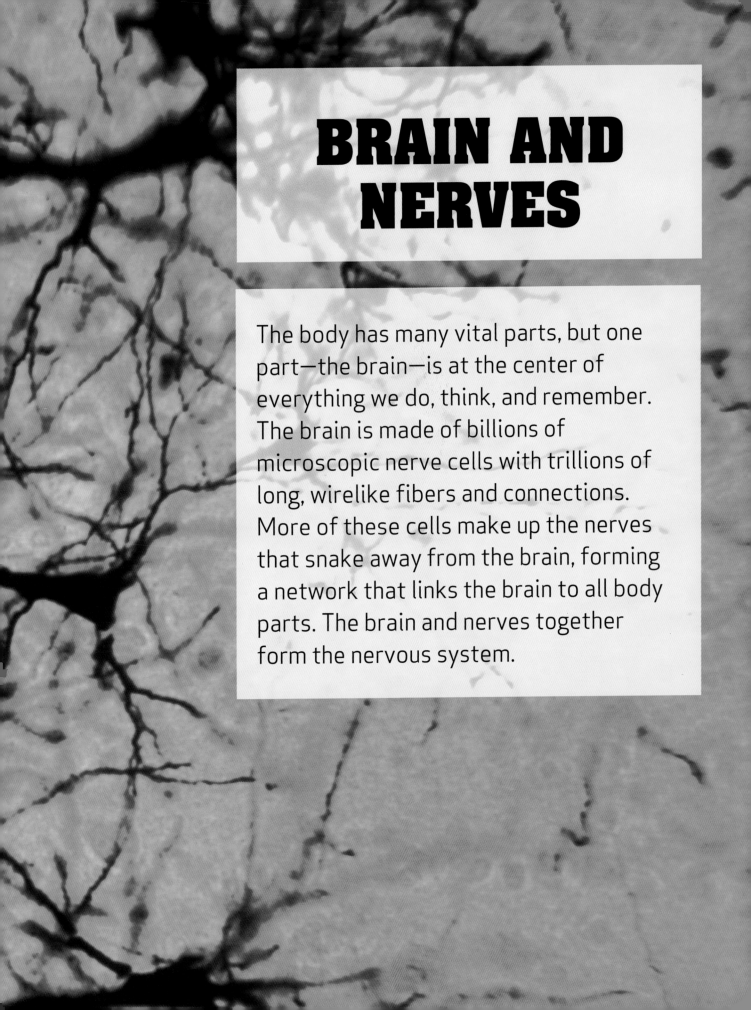

BRAIN AND NERVES

The body has many vital parts, but one part—the brain—is at the center of everything we do, think, and remember. The brain is made of billions of microscopic nerve cells with trillions of long, wirelike fibers and connections. More of these cells make up the nerves that snake away from the brain, forming a network that links the brain to all body parts. The brain and nerves together form the nervous system.

Around the Brain

The brain, perhaps the most precious body part, is soft and slightly floppy, kind of like a pink-gray jelly. It is protected against damage by a hard skull bone and by a special cushioning fluid.

A close-up image showing the wrinkled surface of the brain

Exterior surface of brain

Meninges and Fluid

The brain sits inside the skull and takes up the top half of the head. Inside the skull, three soft membranes called meninges wrap around the brain. Between the inner two meninges is a layer of liquid known as cerebrospinal fluid, or CSF. Together, the meninges and fluid form a soft cushion around the brain.

Top Facts

- The cushioning fluid flows around and inside the brain.
- There are four fluid-filled chambers called ventricles in the brain, which produce CSF.
- The total amount of the cushioning fluid is 4 ounces—roughly half a cup.

Cranium (dome of skull bone)

A cutaway of the skull showing the brain and the four lobes of the cerebrum (see page 130)

It's Amazing!

At birth, the body is only 4 percent of its adult size, but the brain is already about 33 percent of its adult size.

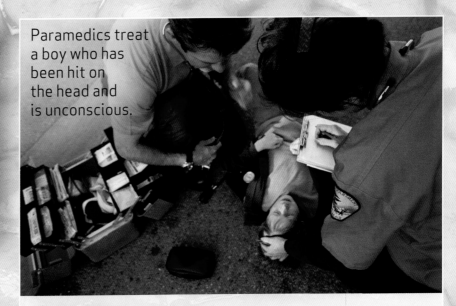

Paramedics treat a boy who has been hit on the head and is unconscious.

Knockout

Someone who has been knocked out, or made unconscious, by a blow to the head does not respond or make any movements and seems to be asleep. There may be a brain injury that will require emergency care.

Bone Dome

Over and around the brain is the dome of the skull bone, called the cranium. This is very strong and guards the brain against bumps and blows. The skin and hair on the head add to this protection and stop the head and brain from getting too hot or cold.

A nurse helps a stroke patient to walk again.

Slow Recovery

During a stroke, a lack of blood to the brain— perhaps caused by a blocked artery—results in brain cells dying. It may take someone a long time to recover from a stroke, because the undamaged parts of the brain have to learn to take over the work from the damaged parts.

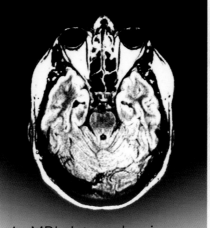

An MRI picture showing a horizontal slice through the middle of the brain

Seeing Inside

A magnetic resonance imaging, or MRI, scanner uses magnetism and radio waves to form an image of thin layers, or slices, of the brain. The images are put together to form a picture of the whole brain to see how it works and to identify any illnesses or problems.

Parts of the Brain

The biggest part of the brain is the cerebrum—the large wrinkled dome at the top. This is where most of our thoughts, feelings, and ideas take place.

When studying math, the left side of the brain is very active.

The four lobes that make up the cerebrum

Parietal lobe

Frontal lobe

Occipital lobe

Temporal lobe

On the Outside

The cerebrum makes up about 90 percent of the brain. It is divided into four regions called lobes, and into left and right halves known as cerebral hemispheres. In most people, the left side of the brain is used for speaking, reading, and figuring out problems. The right side of the brain usually deals with more "artistic" skills, such as painting and imagination. The wrinkled surface of the cerebrum is a thin layer called the cerebral cortex.

In the Middle

The center of the brain, under the cerebrum, is involved in awareness— monitoring what we see, hear, and feel. It also deals with emotions and balance and acts as a relay station. This involves passing messages between the upper and lower brain. It includes parts such as the thalamus and the hypothalamus.

The Lower Brain

At the lower rear of the brain is a wrinkled lump called the cerebellum. This part helps to organize nerve signals going out to the muscles. It helps to make our movements smooth and skillful rather than jerky and clumsy. Like the cerebrum, the cerebellum is divided into two halves: left and right.

It's Amazing!

The brain registers pain from other parts of the body, so that we know when they are hurt. But the brain itself has no pain sensors.

The middle of the brain deals with emotions, such as fear.

Emotions

Strong feelings, such as surprise, shock, fear, and anger, are based in the hypothalamus. This is also the area involved in powerful urges, like thirst and hunger.

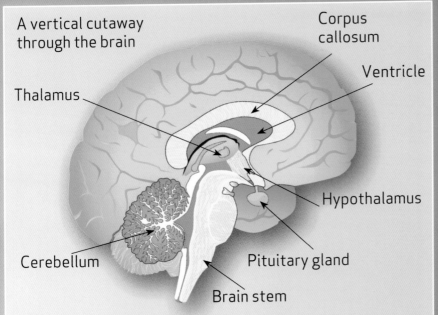

A vertical cutaway through the brain

Corpus callosum

Ventricle

Thalamus

Hypothalamus

Cerebellum

Pituitary gland

Brain stem

On the inside

A cutaway view of the brain reveals its ventricles, or fluid-filled chambers (shown above shaded in blue). Other parts include the egg-shaped thalamus and the hypothalamus, as well as the corpus callosum, which contains millions of nerve fibers that link the left and right sides of the brain. Below all of these is the brain stem, which controls many of the basic life processes, such as breathing, digestion, and blood pressure.

Top Facts

- The average adult brain weighs 3 pounds.

- The largest known normal human brain weighed a whopping 6.5 pounds.

- Bigger brains are not necessarily smarter. There is no link between the size of a healthy brain and a person's intelligence.

Sending Signals

The brain and nerves contain billions of microscopic nerve cells called neurons. These cells are specialized to receive and send information as tiny pulses of electricity called nerve impulses, or nerve signals.

Nerve Cells

A typical nerve cell has a wide body. Branching from this cell are many short, thin fingers called dendrites. There also usually is one longer branch called an axon, or nerve fiber. Nerve messages are picked up by the dendrites, processed and altered as they pass around the cell body, and then sent on by the axon. A motor nerve carries signals to muscles, telling them when to contract. These signals pass along the axon to the muscle fibers. Surrounding some axons is a thick, fatty protective covering called the myelin sheath.

Electronic circuits enable computers to do millions of calculations a second.

Processing Power

Nerve cells work in a similar way to microchips in a computer. Microchips have tiny circuits inside them, along which they send electrical signals.

Dendrite

Nerve cell body

Axon

Myelin sheath surrounds axon

A motor nerve cell

Muscle fibers

Nerve Junctions

The dendrites and axons connect to the dendrites and axons of other nerve cells, but they do not actually touch each other. The junctions are separated by tiny gaps called synapses. Nerve messages "jump" across the synapse— not as electrical signals, but in the form of chemicals called neurotransmitters. Each chemical jump takes less than one thousandth of a second.

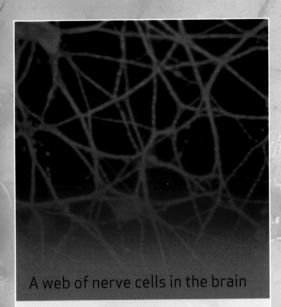

A web of nerve cells in the brain

Nerve Web

The brain contains about 100 billion nerve cells. Each of these may be linked to 10,000 or more other nerve cells. The number of connections means there are trillions of pathways for signals to travel between nerve cells.

It's Amazing!

Brain waves can be detected by sensors on the head that can switch a device on or off. These sensors allow some people who are paralyzed to control devices, such as computers, just by thinking.

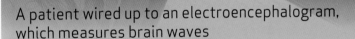

A patient wired up to an electroencephalogram, which measures brain waves

Brain Machine

In 1924, German physician Hans Berger invented the first machine to measure electrical signals in the human brain. In secret, he tried it out on his son, Klaus, then on other people. In 1929, Berger published a report on the brain's electrical activity.

Brain Waves

The brain's electrical signals can be detected by sensor pads on the head. The brain waves, or signals, can then be displayed on a screen or a paper strip as jagged wavy lines. The pattern of waves helps doctors to identify certain brain problems so that they can be treated.

Brain Map

The outer layer of the cerebrum is called the cerebral cortex. It contains about half of the brain's nerve cells—about 50 billion—and the trillions of connections between them.

Bad Accident

In 1848, American railroad worker Phineas Gage suffered a terrible injury. An iron bar passed through his frontal lobe. Before the injury, Gage was likable, but after the injury he became difficult and short-tempered. This event started the study of how the brain is involved in personality and behavior.

A map of the cortex

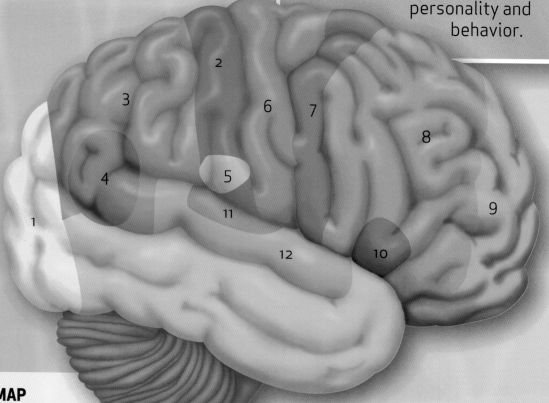

KEY TO BRAIN MAP
1. Visual area (sight)
2. Somatosensory center (touch)
3. Secondary touch area
4. Posterior (Wernicke's) speech center
5. Gustatory center (taste)
6. Motor center (organizing movements)
7. Premotor center (planning movements)
8. Frontal cortex (behavior and personality)
9. Language area (recognizing and understanding words)
10. Anterior (Broca's) speech center
11. Auditory center (hearing)
12. Vestibular center (balance)

Regions of the Cortex

The cortex is where our senses reside. It is the main place in the brain where we become aware of what we see, hear, smell, taste, and touch. It is also the place where we plan movements, known as motor skills, and organize them. Each of these sensory and motor processes takes place in a different area of the cortex.

The brain interprets signals sent by the eyes and turns them into pictures.

Seeing

A person who is hit hard in the lower back of the head, where the visual center is, may have sight problems and "see stars."

It's Amazing!

If the cerebral cortex were spread out flat, it would be the size of a pillowcase and almost as thin. But its deep wrinkles allow it to fit neatly inside the head.

Hearing

Nerve signals from each ear pass along nerves to the hearing center, which is on the temporal lobe. If someone is hit on the head at this place, they sometimes hear buzzing or scratching noises. These sounds do not come from the ear but are "made up" by the jolted brain.

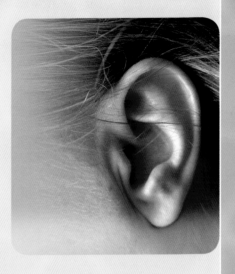

The ears connect directly to the brain via nerves.

The Mind

The cortex is the major site for thinking and for general consciousness, or awareness—what we call our "mind." The cortex is involved in learning and memory, too. It is sometimes called gray matter, because all its nerve cells give it a gray color. Nerve axons from the cortex's nerve cells pass inward to the central part of the brain, where they connect to other parts, such as the thalamus and hypothalamus (see page 131).

Personality

Many parts of the brain are involved in how we behave, how we feel, and what we think. These things make us who we are—or give us our personality. These areas include parts of the cortex, especially the frontal lobe, and the hypothalamus (see pages 130–131). The brain sends signals to your face, maybe telling it to look sad if that's how you feel.

The Main Nerves

Breathing, as this diver is doing underwater, is regulated by the cranial nerves.

The brain cannot do much at all by itself—it depends on nerves to link it to the rest of the body. There are 25 major nerves carrying signals between the brain, the senses, the muscles, and the glands.

Connecting Nerves

The 24 cranial nerves are grouped in 12 pairs. They connect the brain to various parts of the body, mainly in the head and neck. Some carry signals to the brain and are called sensory nerves. Others carry instructions to the muscles and are called motor nerves.

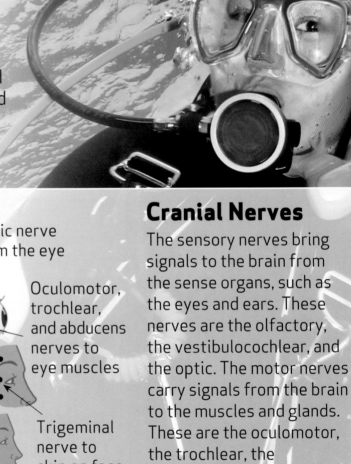

Olfactory nerve from the nose

Optic nerve from the eye

Facial nerve to the tongue, for taste, saliva, and tear glands

Oculomotor, trochlear, and abducens nerves to eye muscles

Vestibulocochlear nerve from the ear, for hearing and balance

Trigeminal nerve to skin on face

Glossopharyngeal nerve to rear tongue, for taste

Accessory nerve to voice box

Hypoglossal nerve to tongue, for speaking and swallowing

Vagus nerve to lungs, heart, and other organs

Cranial Nerves

The sensory nerves bring signals to the brain from the sense organs, such as the eyes and ears. These nerves are the olfactory, the vestibulocochlear, and the optic. The motor nerves carry signals from the brain to the muscles and glands. These are the oculomotor, the trochlear, the abducens, the accessory, and the hypoglossal. Some nerves carry both sensory and motor signals. They are the vagus, the trigeminal, the facial, and the glossopharyngeal.

It's Amazing!

If all the nerves in the body were taken out and connected end to end, they would stretch about 62 miles.

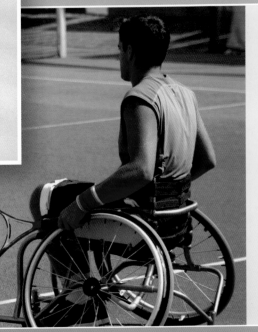

Some people with spinal injuries use wheelchairs to move around.

Spinal Cord

The spinal cord is the brain's chief link to the rest of the body. It starts at the brain stem and passes down into the body via a tunnel along the inside of the backbone. The bones of the spinal column protect the spinal cord from injury.

Spinal Injury

An injury to the neck or back can damage the spinal cord, which may no longer carry signals between the brain and body parts. If the damage is low in the back, it can affect feeling and movement in the legs. If the damage is in the neck, then the arms may also lose feeling and movement.

Top Facts

• Nerve signals pass along the nerves at speeds of up to 394 feet per second.

• The largest nerves can handle about 300 signals every single second.

• A person with a spinal injury who has lost the use of his or her legs is called a paraplegic, and someone who has lost the use of both arms and legs is called a quadriplegic.

The squid is very useful for studying how nerves work.

Giant Nerves

A squid's main nerve cell has a giant axon—a huge nerve fiber as thick as the lead in a pencil. This can easily be studied, cut, joined, and altered to find out how nerves work, how they carry nerve signals, and how they can repair themselves.

Body-Wide Nerves

The brain and the spinal cord together are known as the central nervous system. The body-wide network of nerves that connects to them and branches out to all body parts is the peripheral nervous system.

Spinal Nerves

The spinal cord is about 18 inches long and as thick as your little finger. Like the brain, it has meninges and cerebrospinal fluid around it to cushion it from bumps and hits. Pairs of nerves branch left and right from the cord. These nerves connect to muscles, glands, bones, skin, blood vessels, and other body parts, reaching right to the ends of your fingers and toes.

Tough Nerves

A typical nerve looks like shiny gray string. It is flexible enough to bend at your joints but tough enough to withstand being squeezed by the muscles around it. Inside the nerve are bundles of axons. The widest nerves are the sciatic nerves, which are the major nerves from the legs and are each as thick as a thumb.

Brain

Spinal cord

Thoracic (upper body) nerves

Radial nerve

Median nerve

Ulnar nerve

Sacral (pelvis) nerves

Femoral (upper leg) nerve

Cervical (neck) nerves

The major nerves of the body

To do karate, a person needs quick reaction times.

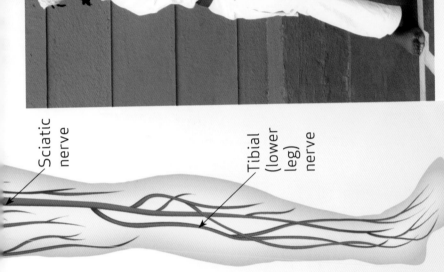

Sciatic nerve

Tibial (lower leg) nerve

Speedy Signals

While the slowest nerve signals travel at about 1.5 feet per second, the fastest can flash from your toes to your brain in less than 0.02 seconds! The speed of nerve signals limits how fast we can react—for example, in sports. The time it takes to react to omething, such as the starting gun in a race, is usually about 0.25 seconds.

It's Amazing!

Nerve signals for pain move slower than those for touch. When you stub your toe, you feel your toe touch something, then a split second later you feel the pain.

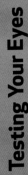

A doctor tests the knee-jerk reflex by tapping the knee.

Reflexes

Some nerves send signals to the spinal cord, which sends signals back without involving the brain. The result is an automatic reaction called a reflex. Doctors check reflexes to make sure nerves are working properly.

Testing Your Eyes

- In a well-lit room, look at one of your eyes in a mirror and notice the size of the pupil. Close both eyes for 10 seconds.
- The instant you open them, watch the pupil carefully. As soon as the eyes open, the pupils get smaller. This is a reflex (see page 153).

Thinking, Learning, and Memory

What is a thought, and where does it happen? Our thoughts and ideas are sets of nerve signals flashing around different pathways in the brain, especially in the cortex.

Pupils learning in class. Facts that you learn go into your memory.

Learning

When we learn something, we form a memory of it. Like thoughts, memories are certain pathways of nerve signals called memory traces. To learn something, nerve cells form synapses, or new connections, to create a new memory trace.

There are two types of memory. Short-term memory involves memories that are stored for only 30 seconds, while long-term memories are stored for much longer.

Where Are Memories Kept?

There is no single memory center in your brain. Some aspects of a memory are stored in the prefrontal part of the cerebral cortex, and some in other brain areas, such as the amygdala. The hippocampus helps to store important memories for a long time.

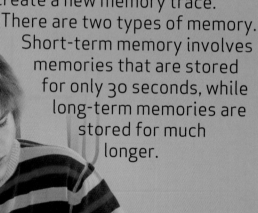

Prefrontal cortex

The external and internal parts of the brain involved in memory

Amygdala

Hippocampus

So Many Memories

Memory is not only used for lists of facts. We remember people's names, events such as birthdays and holidays, how to carry out skilled movements, and many other things. In some ways, memories are like muscles. The more they are used, the stronger they stay. Recalling a memory means that signals pass around the memory trace, refreshing the connections.

It's Amazing!

For its size, the brain uses 10 times more energy than other body parts. The brain uses 20 percent of the body's total energy supply.

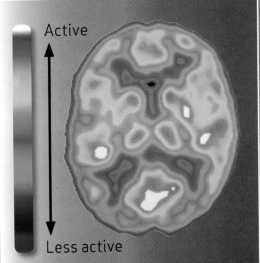

Active

Less active

A PET scan of a cross-section of the brain showing the active areas during a brain stimulation test

Busy Brain

PET (positron emission tomography) scans show which parts of the brain are active during a task or when learning something. The busiest brain parts "light up" because their nerve cells are very active and use more energy.

Memory Games

Look at the objects above for 20 seconds and then close the book and try to remember as many as you can. You will probably be able to recall some of them. By using some of the tricks described on the right, you may recall more and remember them for longer.

Memory Tricks

- In the game on the left, write down the first letter of the name of each object and arrange the letters into a new word.

- Or invent a story that includes the objects.

- Or try grouping them according to their colors. These "tricks" should help to improve your memory.

Good Night's Sleep

For about a third of our lives, we are not aware of our brains at all—this is when we are asleep. But scientific studies of sleeping people show that the brain is busy all night.

Body and Brain

The heartbeat and breathing slow down during sleep. So do digestion and urine production. Most muscles relax. Some processes, however, speed up. Our bodies repair the everyday wear and tear in cells and tissues more quickly at night.

During sleep, most people move around a lot. This stops nerves and blood vessels from being squished.

Sleep Cycle

The first part of a night's sleep is deep sleep (stage 4). After an hour or two, sleep becomes lighter, the eyes move and breathing speeds up. This is REM (rapid eye movement) sleep (stage 1), when dreams occur. Periods of deep and light sleep follow, with the deep sleep becoming shallower (stages 3 and 2) toward morning.

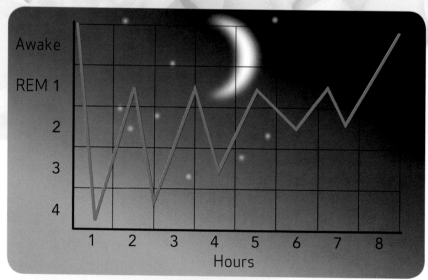

A graph of the different stages of sleep during the night

Top Facts

On average:

- A new baby sleeps for 20 hours a day.

- A 10-year-old sleeps for about 10 hours.

- Most adults sleep for 7 to 8 hours each night.

- Some people can stay healthy on just 5 hours of sleep a night, while others need 10 hours.

Jet Lag

Sleeping occurs in a 24-hour rhythm regulated by the "body clock," which is based in a tiny part of the brain. Your body clock is affected by daylight and darkness. When you travel long distances quickly, your body clock can get confused. This is known as jet lag.

It's Amazing!

In 1964, American student Randy Gardner stayed awake for 11 days, which is a world record. But going without sleep can be very harmful (see right).

Losing Sleep

Exactly what the brain does during sleep is not clear. It may be sorting through the day's events and deciding what to remember or forget. Some people are unable to sleep during the night. This is called insomnia. A lack of sleep can cause tiredness, headaches, confusion, slowed reactions, and many other problems. Serious lack of sleep is linked to accidents, infections, and other illnesses.

Night Shift

Some people work at night, when most of us are asleep. If this happens regularly, the body and brain gradually adjust their sleeping and eating times and settle into a new routine. But switching quickly between daytime and nighttime working has been linked to various health problems.

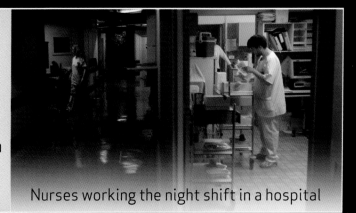

Nurses working the night shift in a hospital

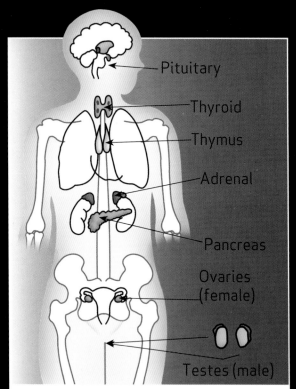

The major endocrine glands

Hormone Glands

Various glands around the body form the endocrine system. These glands make chemicals called hormones and release them into the blood.

Chemical Control

The brain and nerves, which send information as tiny electrical signals, are not the body's only control system. A second system also organizes and controls body parts and processes. It is not electrical but chemical and is called the endocrine, or hormonal, system.

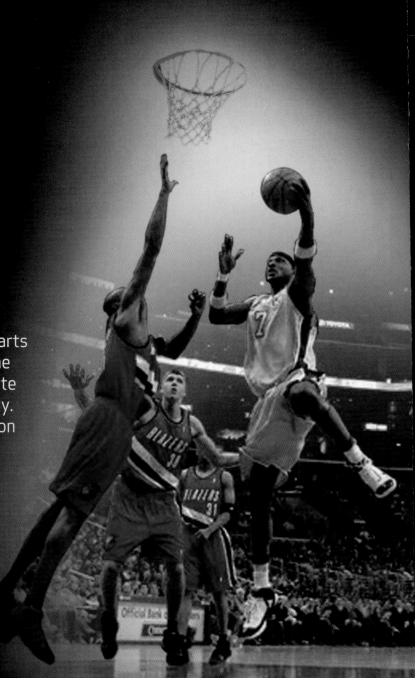

Hormones

Different hormones affect different parts of your body. Hormones released by the thyroid gland in the neck control the rate of many chemical processes in the body. Adrenal hormones affect the production of urine and how you cope with stress. Hormones from the pancreas regulate the level of sugar in the blood.

Growth hormone is made in the pituitary. Higher levels of it make the body grow taller, which is very useful in sports such as basketball.

Diabetes Pioneers

In 1921 in Canada, Frederick Banting and Charles Best discovered insulin—a hormone made by the pancreas. They also found that animal insulin could be used to treat diabetes, a condition in which the body cannot control the levels of sugar found in the blood.

Some people enjoy the "adrenaline rush" of a bungee jump.

Adrenaline Rush

The adrenal glands make adrenaline, which gives the body a burst of energy by increasing the heart rate and flow of blood. This allows the body to react quickly to danger or stress, either by running away or facing it—this is known as fight or flight.

It's Amazing!

Laughter is good for you because it can reduce the levels of stress hormones (such as adrenaline) in your body, making you more relaxed.

The Speed of Control

There are more than 30 main hormones in your body and these control processes that happen fairly slowly—over hours, days, or even years. These processes include growth, digestion, and making urine. In contrast, the processes the nerves control happen much faster—usually over seconds or minutes.

Nerves and Hormones

The pituitary makes more than 10 hormones, many of which control other endocrine glands. For example, it releases a hormone that stimulates the ovaries to produce eggs. The pituitary is linked by blood vessels and nerves to the hypothalamus and the brain. Using these links, the nervous and hormonal systems work together to make the body function normally.

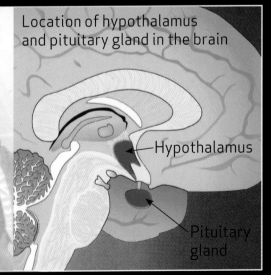

Location of hypothalamus and pituitary gland in the brain

Hypothalamus

Pituitary gland

Brain and Nerve Problems

The brain and nerves do such important jobs that problems with them can be serious. Most people, however, just experience minor problems, such as mild headaches.

Funny Feelings

Sometimes, when we sit or lie in an awkward position, we get a strange tingling feeling called "pins and needles." This is usually a result of squished blood vessels, which reduce blood flow to nerves. When this happens, we cannot feel or move the body part. Bending, stretching, and rubbing the part soon cures the problem.

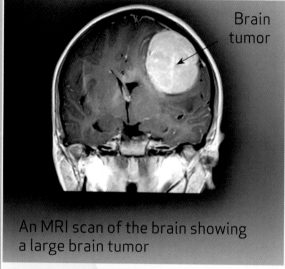

Brain tumor

An MRI scan of the brain showing a large brain tumor

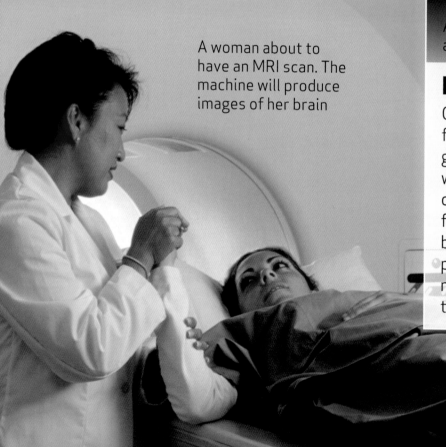

A woman about to have an MRI scan. The machine will produce images of her brain

Brain Tumors

Occasionally, a tumor, or growth, forms inside the brain. As it grows, it squishes the brain within the skull. The pressure can cause headaches and loss of feeling and movement in certain body parts, as well as vision problems and mood swings. It may be possible to cut a hole in the skull and remove the tumor.

Meningitis

Bacteria and viruses can infect the layers around the brain—the meninges. This illness is called meningitis and it causes a severe headache and other symptoms, such as a stiff neck and skin rash. Meningitis is serious and requires emergency treatment.

A magnified image of the bacteria that can cause meningitis

Brain Doctors

- More than 2300 years ago, Greek doctor Hippocrates described the condition of epilepsy and said it was based in the brain.

- Operations on the brain can be performed while the patient is awake, to ensure doctors operate on the correct areas of the brain.

Electrical Storm

Epilepsy is a condition in which nerve signals in the brain are disturbed. Some forms of epilepsy involve short periods of "daydreaming" or making odd movements, such as chewing. In other forms, the person loses consciousness and makes jerky movements called convulsions. Drugs can usually control the problem.

It's Amazing!

In ancient times, people used sharp stones to drill through the skull into the brain, perhaps in an attempt to cure bad headaches. Some people even survived this "treatment"!

Headaches and Migraines

The brain has no pain sensors and cannot feel pain. Headaches usually come from parts around the brain, such as the meninges, blood vessels, and muscles. There may be many causes, including infections and stress. Migraines are severe headaches that keep coming back. Doctors are not sure what causes them.

Almost all people get headaches at some time, but most are not serious.

Guarding the Brain

The brain is well protected by the meninges, cerebrospinal fluid, and skull. But if we do risky activities, such as cycling or rock climbing, it makes good sense to give the brain extra protection.

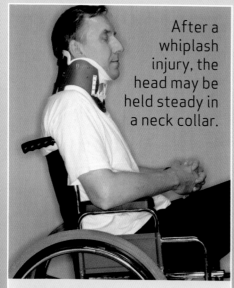

After a whiplash injury, the head may be held steady in a neck collar.

Whiplash

A car accident may cause the head to "whip" backward and forward on the neck. This can bruise and damage the spinal cord and nerves, causing pain and spasms as well as some temporary loss of movement and feeling in the body. This is called whiplash.

Slow to Heal

Nerve cells are very delicate and specialized, and they grow thousands of complex links and connections over many years. If nerve cells are damaged, they are very slow to heal, and sometimes they are not able to repair themselves at all. That is why preventing injuries to the brain and nerves is so important.

A surgeon uses a camera during an operation to project views of the brain onto a screen.

Brain Surgery

Doctors use special saws, drills, and other equipment to open a flap of bone in the skull and expose the brain beneath. Long, thin probes or needles can be pushed deep into the brain to carefully remove diseased tissue or take samples for analysis.

Shields and Guards

Nerves are especially at risk of being damaged where they pass through joints. Joint guards on the elbows and knees help to reduce the risk. If a body part is cut off in an accident, doctors may be able to reconnect it using microsurgery. This is when muscles, blood vessels, and even nerve fibers are rejoined under a microscope.

Wearing a helmet and other protective gear is essential when riding a motorbike.

It's Amazing!

Staying unconscious for a long time, usually after an accident, is called a coma. In 2003, American Terry Wallis, who was 39, woke up after 19 years in a coma. His first word was "Mom."

Growing Nerves

Medical researchers are looking for ways to help repair damaged nerves. Some chemicals, known as neuronal growth factors, encourage nerve cells to lengthen their fibers and send out new connections. Special cells in the nose may have the potential to regenerate into new nerve cells if transplanted into the spine.

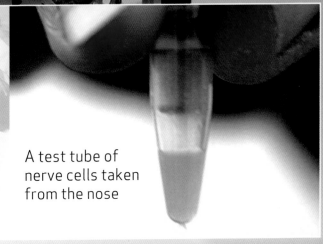

A test tube of nerve cells taken from the nose

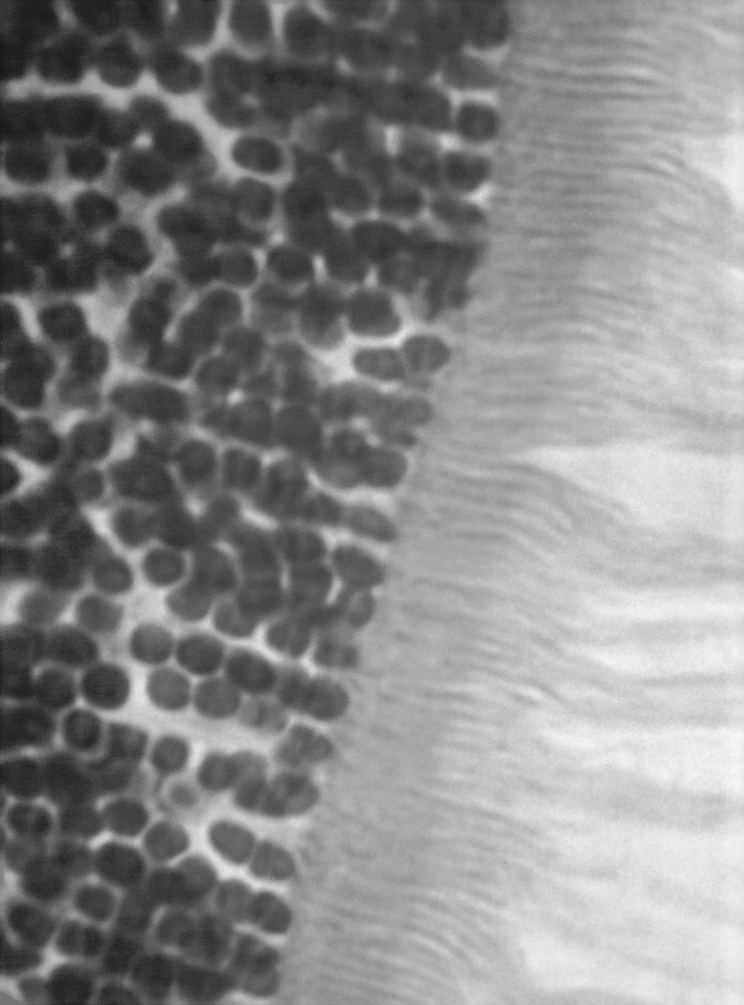

THE SENSES

Can you remember an exciting event such as a theme-park ride, carnival, or music show? Take a moment to recall the bright lights, the sounds of the people, machines, and music, and the things you touched. You might also remember the different smells that were in the air and perhaps the taste of a snack or treat. Your body's sensory systems—sight, hearing, smell, taste, and touch—allow you to experience all these wonderful things.

The Eyes

It is thought that more than half of the information in our brains comes through our eyes—as words, photographs, drawings, real-life scenes, and images on screens.

It's Amazing!

The eye grows less than any other body part from birth to adulthood. It is already about 70 percent of its adult size at birth. This is why babies seem to have such big eyes.

Ball and Socket

Each eyeball is protected by an orbit, or eye socket—a cone-shaped cavity in the skull. The eyeball is ball-shaped and measures about 1 inch across. Only about one eighth of the eyeball is visible at the front.

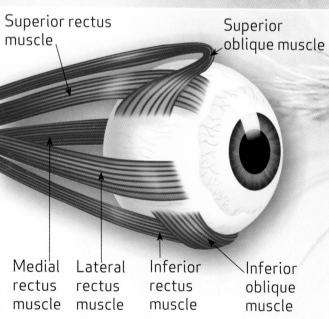

Superior rectus muscle

Superior oblique muscle

Medial rectus muscle

Lateral rectus muscle

Inferior rectus muscle

Inferior oblique muscle

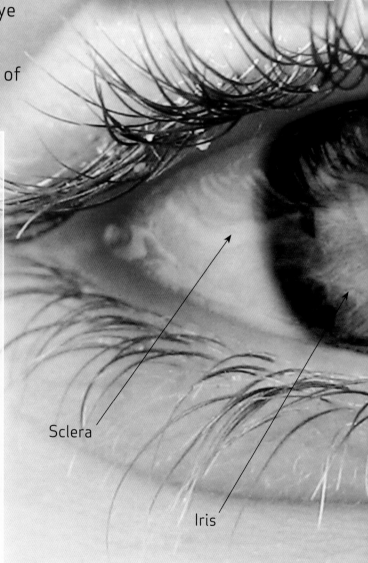

Sclera

Iris

Moving the Eye

Six long, slim, ribbonlike muscles connect to different parts of the eyeball. Working as a team, these move the eyeball to look up or down and left or right. The eye muscles are among the fastest-reacting in the body.

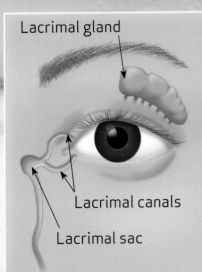

Lacrimal gland

Lacrimal canals

Lacrimal sac

Making Tears

Tear fluid is made in the lacrimal glands above each eyeball. Tears smear over the surface of the eyeball with each blink and wash away dust and germs. They then flow through two tubes to a pouch called the lacrimal sac and into the nose.

A crying baby

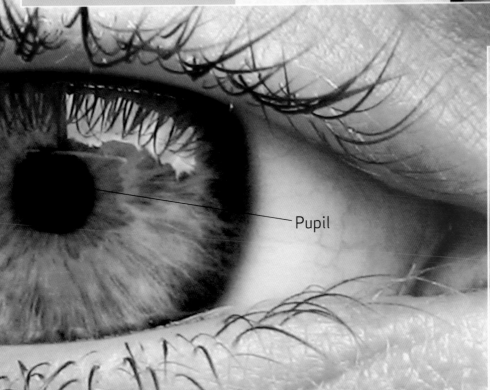

Pupil

Normal light

Bright light

Dim light

Front of the Eye

The most noticeable part of the eye is a ring of pigmented cells called the iris, which varies in color from person to person. In the middle is the pupil, which looks like a black dot but is actually a hole that lets light into the eye's interior. Around the iris is the white of the eye—a tough outer covering of the eyeball called the sclera.

Pupil Response

The muscles of the iris relax or contract to change the size of the pupil. The pupil widens in dim light to let in as much light as possible. In bright light, the pupil narrows to prevent too much light entering.

The Ears

We do not hear with the ears on the sides of our head. These are simply flaps of skin and cartilage. Sounds are changed to nerve signals by a part inside the ear called the cochlea.

A diagram of the ear, showing the outer ear and a cutaway of the middle and inner ear

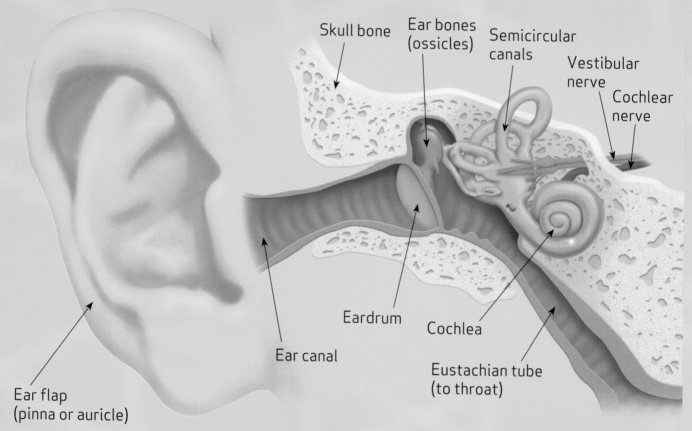

Skull bone

Ear bones (ossicles)

Semicircular canals

Vestibular nerve

Cochlear nerve

Eardrum

Cochlea

Ear canal

Eustachian tube (to throat)

Ear flap (pinna or auricle)

Ear Flaps

The ear flaps help to gather sound waves from the air and guide them into the ear canal. Their shape also helps to keep dust, dirt, and other objects out of the ear. The canal's lining of wax also traps dust.

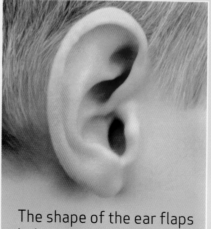

The shape of the ear flaps helps to trap sound.

Parts of the Ear

The ear has three main sections. The outer ear is the ear flap on the side of the head and a tube—the ear canal—leading from it. The middle ear is the eardrum at the end of the ear canal and three tiny ear bones. The inner ear is the snail-shaped cochlea and the semicircular canals.

A Look in the Ear

Medical staff can check for ear infections or other problems by shining a light from an otoscope into the ear canal. The earlobe is usually pulled gently to make the ear canal straighter to reveal the eardrum with the ear bones behind it.

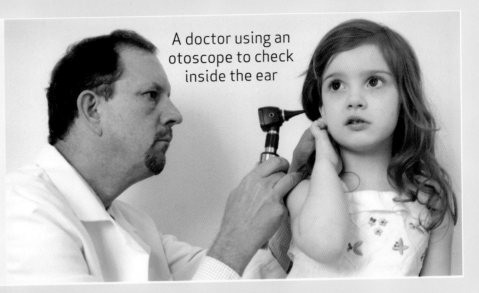

A doctor using an otoscope to check inside the ear

It's Amazing!

Some animals, such as dogs and bats, can hear sounds that humans cannot detect. Some dog whistles seem to make no noise, but dogs can hear them!

Noticing Sounds

Almost nowhere is truly silent. There are usually sounds of some kind—distant traffic, humming machinery, people talking, birds singing, or the wind. Much of the time we ignore these sounds because they tell us nothing new. The ears receive them, but our conscious thoughts do not register them. Only when we hear something new, important, or exciting do we turn our attention to listening.

A bat-eared fox has huge ear flaps, which it uses to locate insects to eat.

Direction of Sound

Many animals have large ears that can be turned to locate a sound. Humans figure out the direction of a sound by hearing if the sound is louder on one side of the head than the other, and if a sound arrives at one ear before the other— even if this difference is a fraction of a second.

Top Facts

- A sound's pitch— whether it sounds high or low—is measured in hertz.

- Human ears can hear a range of sounds, from low sounds at about 25 hertz to very high sounds at about 20,000 hertz.

Nose and Smell

Smell and taste are both known as chemosenses. This means that they detect chemical substances in the form of tiny particles too small to see. The nose reacts to smelly particles, called odorants, floating in the air.

Sniff, Sniff

Odorant particles floating in the air drift into the nose as air is breathed in. They are detected by two olfactory patches in the roof of the nasal chamber. Sniffing something makes air swirl around inside the nose, which brings more odorant particles higher into the nasal chamber, where they touch the olfactory patches.

A flower produces odorant particles to attract insects so that it can be pollinated.

It's Amazing!

The human nose is so sensitive that it can tell the difference between about 10,000 different scents.

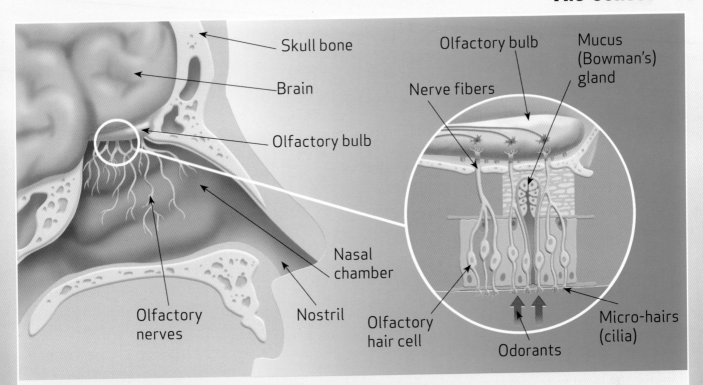

Skull bone

Brain

Olfactory bulb

Olfactory nerves

Nasal chamber

Nostril

Olfactory hair cell

Nerve fibers

Olfactory bulb

Mucus (Bowman's) gland

Micro-hairs (cilia)

Odorants

Inside the Nose

The two nostrils lead into the nasal chamber—the air space inside the nose. Each olfactory patch in the roof of the nasal chamber contains about 10 million olfactory hair cells. These hair cells have about 10 to 20 micro-hairs each. The micro-hairs point down into the thick layer of slimy mucus that lines the inside of the nasal chamber.

A close-up of an olfactory patch, where smells are turned into nerve signals

Smell Receptors

Odorant particles seep into the mucus coating the nasal chamber. They come into contact with the micro-hairs of the olfactory hair cells, and these create nerve signals. The signals are sent to the brain via the olfactory bulb. The brain interprets these signals as the aromas we smell.

Useful Smells

The brain matches a smell to information it has stored about smells. For example, a wine taster can tell what type of wine he or she is about to drink just by sniffing it—and can even tell the year it was made.

A wine taster smelling wine

Tongue and Taste

The tongue works in a way similar to the nose. It detects substances called flavorants in foods and drinks, using tiny taste buds located in bumps called papillae on its surface.

The Tongue's Surface

The tongue has groups of small, pimple-like papillae on its surface, which make it rough so it can grip food. The largest ones are vallate papillae at the rear of the tongue. Other types are the long foliate papillae, the threadlike filiform papillae, and the mushroom-shaped fungiform papillae.

It's Amazing!

Over the years, some taste buds die and are not replaced. This means that younger people are more sensitive to taste than older people are.

Taste Buds

Scattered along the upper sides, tip, and back of the tongue are about 10,000 taste buds. Each contains 20 to 30 gustatory (taste) hair cells, whose micro-hairs stick up into a taste pore in the tongue's surface. Flavorants attach to these hairs and make the hair cells produce nerve signals.

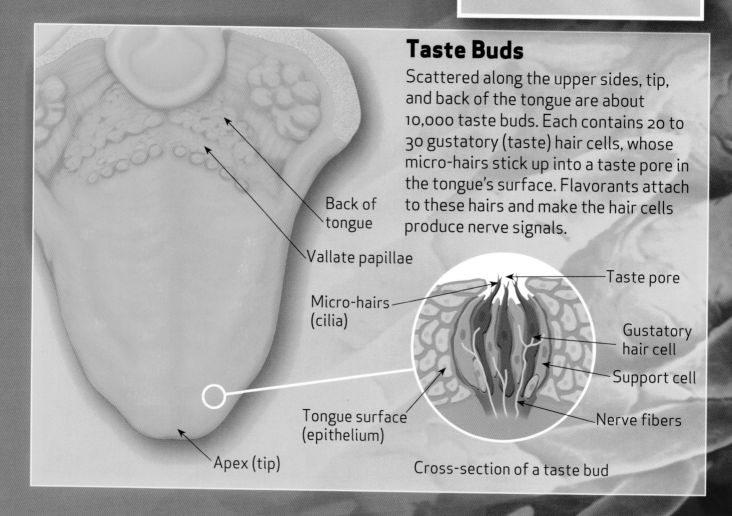

Back of tongue

Vallate papillae

Micro-hairs (cilia)

Taste pore

Gustatory hair cell

Support cell

Nerve fibers

Tongue surface (epithelium)

Apex (tip)

Cross-section of a taste bud

Vallate papilla

Tasting Food

The taste buds work in a way similar to the way olfactory patches work in the nose. They send nerve signals to the gustatory center in the brain (see page 134), which figures out what flavor you are tasting. Your senses of taste and smell work together to determine the flavor. If you have a cold that has blocked your nose, you may notice that the food you eat seems to have less taste. It has the same taste, but you can't smell it as well, so it seems to have less overall flavor.

Magnified view of tongue papillae

Filiform papilla

Strong Flavors

You can sense many different flavors. These are usually grouped into five categories—sweet, salty, sour, bitter, and savory (also called umami)—but there may be more, including spicy flavors such as those found in chilies.

Chilies produce a chemical that creates a burning sensation.

New Thinking

For many years, it was thought that different parts of the tongue sensed different flavors. Recent research shows that most parts of the tongue detect most flavors, except for the central part of the tongue, which has no taste buds.

Skin and Touch

Our sense of touch, or feeling, is more complicated than it seems. It is not single sensory, detecting only physical contact, but is multisensory, feeling many different things.

Skin Structure

Touch is based in the skin, where there are millions of sensors. As the sensors change size or shape, as a result of being squished, vibrated, or expanded by heat, they produce nerve signals that are sent to the somatosensory cortex in the brain (see page 162).

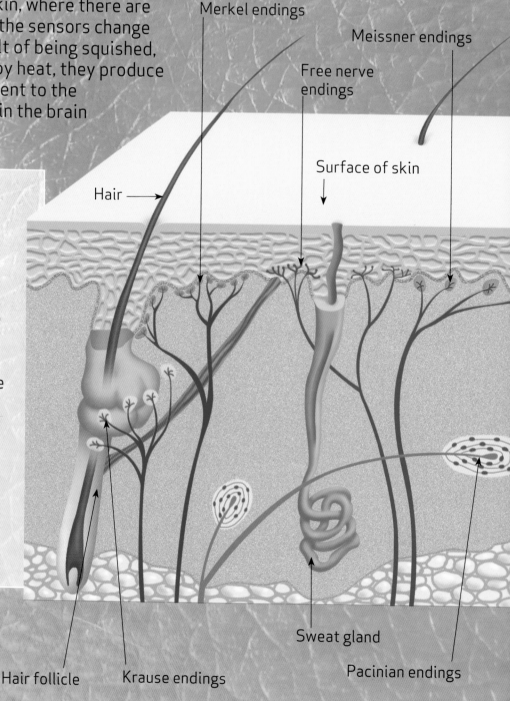

Merkel endings

Meissner endings

Free nerve endings

Surface of skin

Hair

In the Skin

The largest touch sensors are called Pacinian endings. They have many layers like tiny onions and they are 0.02 inches across. The smallest sensors are 100 times tinier than the Pacinian endings. All of these different nerve endings combine to detect a wide range of sensations, including differences in temperature, pressure, vibrations, and pain.

Hair follicle

Krause endings

Sweat gland

Pacinian endings

Scratching

When you feel an itch, your first impulse is to scratch it. Scratching is an important defense mechanism to protect the skin. The itch could be caused by a tick trying to burrow into your skin, and the scratching will knock the tiny creature off before it can dig in.

A magnified image of a tick

Top Facts

- The most touch-sensitive areas of skin include the lips and fingertips. Skin on the fingertips has more than 19,000 touch sensors per square inch.

- The least sensitive areas are the small of the back and the outer thighs.

- The tongue has touch sensors that tell us about the texture of food.

It's Amazing!

A patch of skin the size of a fingernail may contain more than 1,000 touch sensors and 1.5 feet of nerve fibers.

A cross-section through the skin. The touch sensors (all called "endings") are mostly in the top 0.08 inches of skin.

Tickling

No one knows why tickling makes us laugh, but this reaction depends greatly on our mood. If we are happy, we laugh when tickled. If we are worried or sad, then tickling can irritate and upset us.

The feet are very sensitive to tickling.

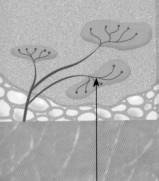

Ruffini endings

Senses in the Brain

The main sensing parts of the body—the eyes, ears, nose, tongue, and skin—send nerve signals to the brain. It is only in the brain that we become aware of what we see, hear, smell, taste, and touch.

Sense Centers

The part of the brain that deals with nerve signals from the skin is called the somatosensory, or touch, center. This is located on the outer layer of the brain—the cerebral cortex. Different body parts send signals to different parts of this center. The more sensitive the skin, the larger the cortex area that receives its signals.

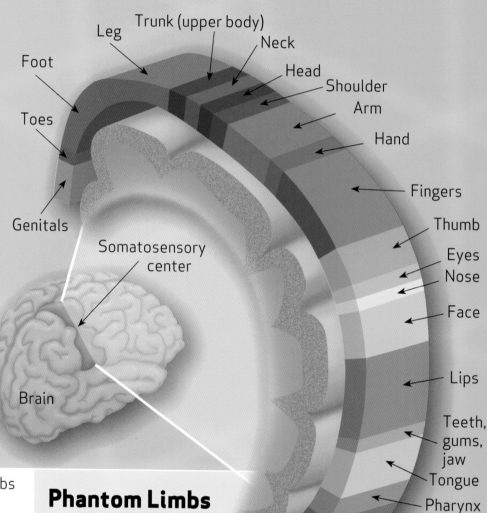

Foot
Toes
Genitals
Somatosensory center
Brain
Leg
Trunk (upper body)
Neck
Head
Shoulder
Arm
Hand
Fingers
Thumb
Eyes
Nose
Face
Lips
Teeth, gums, jaw
Tongue
Pharynx
Intestines

A brain map showing where the different sensory centers for the parts of the body are located and how big they are

People with amputated limbs may still feel pain as if the limb were still there.

Phantom Limbs

Sometimes a limb is so badly damaged that it has to be amputated, or removed. The nerves are cut, but the nerve endings often still make signals. The brain may interpret these as coming from the missing limb.

Going upside down on a roller coaster is scary because your senses are confused.

Sense Overload

A theme-park ride overwhelms the senses with new sights, feelings, and experiences. The senses are thrown into chaos as they try to cope with the body being flung from side to side and upside down.

Putting it Together

Like touch, each of the senses has a center on the cortex (see pages 134–135). These centers constantly communicate with each other by sending nerve signals between themselves. There are also areas that add together the sensory information coming into the brain. These areas give a more complete picture, combining sights, sounds, smells, and other senses to form the memory of an experience.

It's Amazing!

Some people have a condition called synesthesia in which the senses are mixed up. They hear colors, feel sights, and smell tastes!

Brain History

In 1808, German scientist Franz Joseph Gall was the first to suggest that different parts of the brain deal with different senses. In the 20th century, Canadian Wilder Penfield and American Theodore Rasmussen worked out a sensory map of the brain.

Soothing Sense

Senses can greatly affect our mood. If the skin feels something rough, it puts us on edge. But stroking something soft and warm, such as a pet, creates nerve signals that can have a soothing effect.

Petting a cat can make you feel happy.

Inner Senses

The body has many more senses than just the five main ones. Inside the body, there are microscopic sensors that detect blood content, temperature, the position of the joints, and many other things.

Stretch and Strain

Muscles have tiny stretch sensors in them that respond to changes in length and to the amount of tension they are under. These sensors are called neuromuscular spindles. They tell the brain the position of the body and limbs, so that we know this information without having to look. This sense is known as proprioceptive or positional sense.

It's Amazing!

Using the body's positional sense, some complicated movements become almost automatic. Many people can tie their shoelaces without looking, even when talking at the same time!

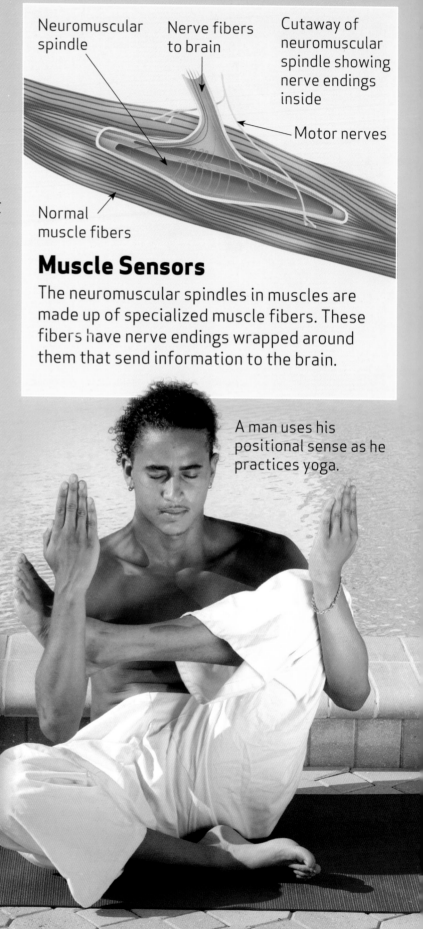

Neuromuscular spindle

Nerve fibers to brain

Cutaway of neuromuscular spindle showing nerve endings inside

Motor nerves

Normal muscle fibers

Muscle Sensors

The neuromuscular spindles in muscles are made up of specialized muscle fibers. These fibers have nerve endings wrapped around them that send information to the brain.

A man uses his positional sense as he practices yoga.

Finger Touch Test

- In a safe place, close your eyes and hold your hands out in front of you.
- Point the index finger of each hand and slowly move your hands so that the tips of your fingers touch.
- You should be able to do this without looking by using your positional sense.

A boy drinks water because his senses have detected that his body needs water.

Chemical Sensors

Sensors in the brain and main blood vessels, called chemoreceptors, monitor the levels of certain substances in the blood. These include oxygen, carbon dioxide, and glucose (sugar). If carbon dioxide rises and oxygen falls, the brain tells us to breathe faster and deeper. These actions will take in extra oxygen and remove more carbon dioxide. This type of response happens automatically as part of the autonomic nervous system.

Fluid Levels

If the monitoring sensors in your body report that the levels of some chemicals, such as salts, in your blood are rising, it means the amount of water in your blood has become too low. To deal with this problem, the brain's hypothalamus makes you feel thirsty and want to have a drink.

Body Thermostat

The main sensors for body temperature are in the hypothalamus. These sensors monitor the temperature of blood as it flows from the heart to the brain. If the temperature rises, the hypothalamus triggers various reactions to lower it. These include flushed skin, flattened skin hairs, and sweating (see page 17).

Sweating is just one of the methods the body uses to maintain body temperature.

Staying Balanced

Balance is sometimes called the sixth sense, but it is not really a single sense. It is a continual process of receiving information from several senses and then adjusting the body's muscles to stay steady and not fall over.

Ears and Balance

Some information about balance comes from the inner ears. Each inner ear contains semicircular canals and two chambers—the utricle and saccule. The utricle and saccule monitor the position of the head by detecting which way is up, then send nerve signals to the brain.

A gymnast balances on a narrow, wooden balance beam.

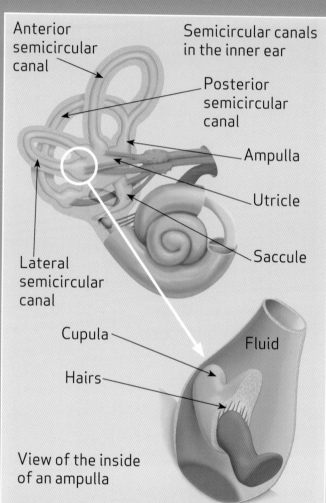

Anterior semicircular canal

Semicircular canals in the inner ear

Posterior semicircular canal

Ampulla

Utricle

Saccule

Lateral semicircular canal

Cupula

Fluid

Hairs

View of the inside of an ampulla

Semicircular Canals

At one end of each fluid-filled canal is a pouch called the ampulla. This contains a jellylike blob, the cupula, which has micro-hairs from hair cells sticking into it. As the head turns, the fluid moves the cupula and the micro-hairs. The hair cells then send signals to the brain.

Unsteady Surroundings

In a boat on rough seas, the body is thrown around in an unnatural way. The brain has problems putting together the strange information coming from the inner ears, eyes, skin, muscles, and other sensing parts. This can cause feelings of dizziness, nausea, and even vomiting, which is called motion sickness or seasickness.

Many people who travel in boats get seasick. They can take certain medicines that help to make them feel better.

It's Amazing!

In 2002, Daniel Baraniuk managed to spend 196 days balanced on a small platform at the top of a pole. Luckily, he had a short break every two hours.

More Balance Input

Information about balance also comes from the eyes. They can see whether the body is the right way up. Information is also sent by the muscles and joints about the limb positions (see page 164). The brain puts together all this information and then controls various muscles to keep the body in balance.

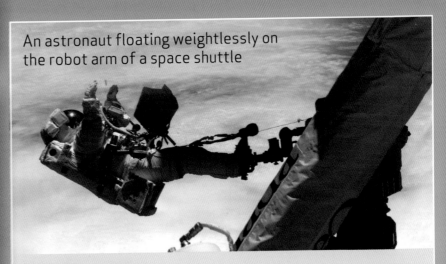

An astronaut floating weightlessly on the robot arm of a space shuttle

Balancing Test

- In a safe place, stand upright with your arms at your sides and close your eyes. Without the information from your eyes, you may feel a bit unsteady.

- Now, stand on one leg. This makes you even less able to balance. Warning: Open your eyes if you feel like you might fall over.

No Weight

In space, where there is no gravity, the brain does not receive normal information from the inner ears about which way is up. This can lead to feelings of sickness, dizziness, confusion, and headaches. These feelings, known as SAS (Space Adaptation Syndrome), or space sickness, usually pass after a few days.

Eye and Ear Problems

Any problems that affect the eyes and ears also affect our ability to communicate with other people. New technologies, such as laser eye surgery and electronic hearing aids, help many people to overcome these difficulties.

A group of children learning to communicate using sign language

It's Amazing!
A horse can hear sounds that are five times quieter than the human ear can detect.

Sign Language
People who cannot hear from a young age are unable to listen to others speaking or to the sound of their own voice. This means that they will have problems learning to speak. Sign language allows people who cannot hear to communicate using their fingers and hands—as well as their arms, bodies, and facial expressions. These "signs" combine to represent various words and phrases.

Most hearing aids fit into the ear and are hardly noticeable.

Hearing Aids

People who can't hear well, especially if their problem is caused by old age, often wear hearing aids. These change the sound waves into electrical signals and play them back as louder sound waves into the ears.

Top Facts

- Cataracts are the most common cause of blindness.

- The most common hearing problems are caused by infections—when germs multiply in the ear. In "glue ear," the infection causes a sticky fluid that stops the ear bones from vibrating.

Sight Problems

Common sight problems include cataracts and glaucoma. In glaucoma, the pressure of fluid inside the eye rises and squeezes the retina and nerve fibers. Drugs and surgery are the main treatments for both of these conditions.

Short and Long Sight

Short sight is when the eyeball is too long, and the lens focuses images of distant objects in front of the retina. This means only near objects can be seen clearly. Long sight is the opposite—the eyeball is too short, meaning that images of near objects are focused behind the retina, so only distant objects are seen clearly.

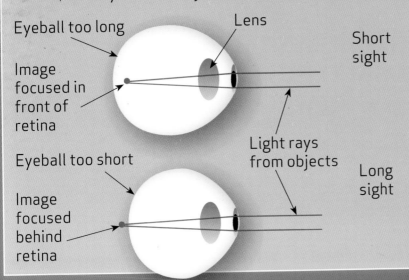

Eyeball too long

Lens

Short sight

Image focused in front of retina

Eyeball too short

Light rays from objects

Long sight

Image focused behind retina

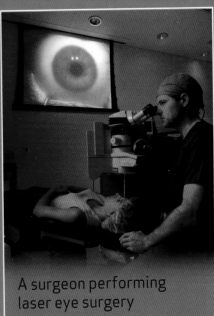

A surgeon performing laser eye surgery

Eye Surgery

Some eye surgery is done with lasers. These shave away parts of the lens or cornea so that rays of light are bent correctly and images focus on the retina.

Protecting the Senses

Just a moment with your eyes closed and your hands over your ears shows you how important seeing and hearing are. It is vital to protect these precious senses from damage.

Sunglasses protect the eyes, but even with them on you should never look directly at the sun.

Too Much Sun

Our eyes are very delicate and easily harmed—not only by physical dangers, such as pieces of grit, but also by bright light. Strong sunshine can damage the retina, so sunglasses should always be worn on sunny days. Most sunglasses have special materials that filter out harmful rays in sunlight.

Correcting Eyesight

Short or long sight (see page 169) can usually be corrected by wearing glasses or contact lenses. These curved pieces of clear glass or plastic bend the light rays from an object so that the image is focused correctly on the retina and can be seen clearly.

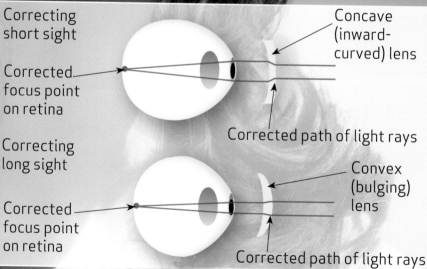

Correcting short sight

Corrected focus point on retina

Concave (inward-curved) lens

Corrected path of light rays

Correcting long sight

Corrected focus point on retina

Convex (bulging) lens

Corrected path of light rays

It's Amazing!

The world's biggest eyes belong to the giant squid and are nearly as large as soccer balls. The largest ears are on the African elephant and are almost the size of an office desk.

Guarding the Eyes

People who use welding torches create sparks and flying particles that can damage the eyes. Welders must wear goggles or visors to protect the eyes from sparks, and also from the brightness of the flames.

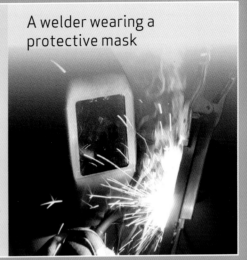

A welder wearing a protective mask

Protecting Your Hearing

Loud noise that goes on for a long time, especially if it is high-pitched, can gradually affect the hearing. If the delicate nerve endings and hair cells of the cochlea in the ear are damaged by loud noise, it is difficult to repair them. You should avoid listening to music with the volume too high for too long, especially on your headphones.

Guarding the Ears

Safety earmuffs stop very loud noises from harming the inner ear. They should be worn when using noisy equipment, such as chain saws, and when working in noisy environments, such as in factories and airports.

A builder wears safety earmuffs to protect his hearing when cutting stone.

Vision Firsts

The first eyeglasses were invented in Italy in the late 13th century. Glass contact lenses were developed in the 1880s, but they were big and heavy. Plastic contact lenses arrived in the 1940s, but the plastic was hard. During the 1950s, soft plastic contact lenses were invented.

INDEX

ACKNOWLEDGMENTS

Artwork supplied through the Art Agency by Terry Pastor, Barry Croucher, Robin Carter, and Dave Smith

Photo credits:
b = bottom, t = top, r = right, l = left, c = center

Front cover: tl John_Woodcock/Getty, tr PIXOLOGICSTUDIO/Getty, c Shutterstock, br iStock, bc and bl Sebastian Kaulitzki/Getty
Back cover: tr iStock, br Laguna Design/Getty, b Science Photo Library/PASIEKA/Getty, l iStock

1 Dreamstime.com, 2-3 William Attard Mccarthy/Dreamstime.com, 3c Dreamstime.com, 4-5 Zena Holloway/zefa/Corbis, 8-9 Micro Discovery/Corbis, 10-11 William Attard Mccarthy/Dreamstime.com, 10cl Anette Linnea Rasmussen/Dreamstime.com, 10cr Dreamstime.com, 11tl Pierre Lahalle/TempSport/Corbis, 12-13 Visuals Unlimited/Corbis, 13tr Ljupco Smokovski/Dreamstime.com, 14-15 Gabe Palmer/zefa/Corbis, 14l Dreamstime.com, 15tr Dreamstime.com, 16-17 Fritz Langmann/Dreamstime.com, 17tr S. Carmona/CORBIS, 18-19 Visuals Unlimited/Corbis, 19tr Reuters/CORBIS, 20-21 Dreamstime.com, 20bl Karen Struthers/Dreamstime.com, 21tr Dreamstime.com, 21bl Jonathan Pais/ Dreamstime.com, 22-23 Anthony Redpath/CORBIS, 23tr Mediscan/Corbis, 23bl Dreamstime.com, 24-25 Fendis/zefa/Corbis, 25tr Visuals Unlimited/Corbis, 25bl Anke Van Wyk/Dreamstime.com, 26-27 Susanne Dittrich/zefa/Corbis, 26cl Anna Moller/zefa/Corbis, 27br Jaimie Duplass/Dreamstime.com, 28-29 Lester V. Bergman/CORBIS, 29br Wendy Kaveney/Dreamstime.com, 30-31 Grace/zefa/Corbis, 30c Visuals Unlimited/Corbis, 31tr Rob Marmion/Dreamstime.com, 31bl Carolina k. Smith m.d./Dreamstime.com, 32-33 Visuals Unlimited/Corbis, 34tc Dreamstime.com, 35bl Bettmann/CORBIS, 36-37 and 37bl Lester V. Bergman/CORBIS, 36cl Lester V. Bergman/CORBIS, 38-39 Geir-olav Lyngfjell/Dreamstime.com, 39tl Dreamstime.com, 39bc Manuela Krause/Dreamstime.com, 40-41 Duomo/CORBIS, 40bl all Dreamstime.com, 41cr Dreamstime.com, 41bc Dreamstime.com, 42-43 Lester V. Bergman/CORBIS, 42cr Dreamstime.com, 43br Lester V. Bergman/CORBIS, 44-45 Linda Bucklin/Dreamstime.com, 44 Janet Carr/Dreamstime.com, 45tc Oleg Kozlov/Dreamstime.com, 45cr Rod Ferris/Dreamstime.com, 46-47 and 46br Ron Boardman; Frank Lane Picture Agency/CORBIS, 47tr Sue Colvil/Dreamstime.com, 47cl Dreamstime.com, 48-49 Sean Nel/Dreamstime.com, 49tr Dreamstime.com, 49br Anton Novozhilov/Dreamstime.com, 51br Dreamstime.com, 52-53 Eddy Lemaistre/Photo & Co./Corbis, 53tl Marek Tihelka/Dreamstime.com, 53cl Dreamstime.com, 54-55 Michael DeYoung/Corbis, 54cl Lester V. Bergman/CORBIS, 55cr Anneke Schram/Dreamstime.com, 56-57 Ben Welsh/zefa/Corbis, 58cl Graça Victoria/Dreamstime.com, 58br Dreamstime.com, 59tr Jaimie Duplass/Dreamstime.com, 59b Katrina Brown/Dreamstime.com, 60-61 Dreamstime.com, 61tr Pete Saloutos/zefa/Corbis, 61br David Badenhorst/Dreamstime.com, 62-63 Najlah Feanny/Corbis, 63tr Lester V. Bergman/CORBIS, 64-65 Lester V. Bergman/CORBIS, 65br Mediscan/Corbis, 66-67 Visuals Unlimited/Corbis, 67tr Lester V. Bergman/CORBIS, 69tr Sonya Etchison/Dreamstime.com, 69br Roman Milert/Dreamstime.com, 70-71 Awilli/zefa/Corbis, 71cl John Sartin/Dreamstime.com, 71tr Randy Faris/Corbis, 72-73 Stephen Sweet/Dreamstime.com, 73cr Mediscan/Corbis, 73br Will Moneymaker/Dreamstime.com, 74-75 Karen Kasmauski/CORBIS, 74bc Micro Discovery/Corbis, 75cr Peter Elvidge/Dreamstime.com, 75bc Bob Sacha/Corbis, 76-77 Etienne Poupinet/zefa/Corbis, 76bl Michael DeYoung/Corbis, 77tl Franz Pfluegl/Dreamstime.com, 77br Jozsef Szasz-fabian/Dreamstime.com, 78-79 Visuals Unlimited/Corbis, 80cl Ioana Grecu/Dreamstime.com, 81bl Howard Sochurek/CORBIS, 84tl Tim Pannell/Corbis, 84-85 Dreamstime.com, 85bl Galina Barskaya/Dreamstime.com, 86-87 Sebastian Kaulitzki/Dreamstime.com, 87br Wa Li/Dreamstime.com, 88-89 Wa Li/Dreamstime.com, 90bl Eugene Bochkarev/Dreamstime.com, 91tc Visuals Unlimited/Corbis, 91br Dreamstime.com, 92-93 Shutterstock, 93cr Mediscan/Corbis, 93bc Heng kong Chen/Dreamstime.com, 95br Dreamstime.com, 96-97 Visuals Unlimited/Corbis, 98tr Jaimie Duplass/Dreamstime.com, 98b Reuters/CORBIS, 99cl Matthew Mcvay/CORBIS, 100b Jeremy Horner/Corbis, 101tr Dreamstime.com, 101br Peggy Laflesh/Dreamstime.com, 102-103 Klaus Hackenberg/zefa/Corbis, 104r Dreamstime.com, 105cr Jason Stitt/Dreamstime.com, 105bc Gert Vrey/Dreamstime.com, 106r Olga Lyubkina/Dreamstime.com, 107tr Dreamstime.com, 107cr Ryan Pike/Dreamstime.com, 107bc Nicolas Nadjar/Dreamstime.com, 108l Linda Bucklin/Dreamstime.com, 108br Paul Moore/Dreamstime.com, 109br Dreamstime.com, 110-111 Don Mason/Corbis, 112-113 and 113tl Lester V. Bergman/CORBIS, 113tr Dreamstime.com, 113bl Howard Sochurek/CORBIS, 114-115 Micro Discovery/Corbis, 116-117 Dreamstime.com, 117t Howard Sochurek/CORBIS, 117br Dreamstime.com, 118-119 Visuals Unlimited/Corbis, 119cr Peter Jobst/Dreamstime.com, 120-121 Lester V. Bergman/CORBIS, 121cr Tim Graham/Corbis, 123cr Tomasz Trojanowski/Dreamstime.com, 124-125 Dreamstime.com, 125tr Laurent Hamels/Dreamstime.com, 126-127 Lester V. Bergman/CORBIS, 129tr Ronnie Kaufman/Dreamstime.com, 129cl Everett Kennedy Brown/epa/Corbis, 129bc Dreamstime.com, 130 Bob Rowan; Progressive Image/CORBIS, 130cl Dreamstime.com, 131tr Roger Bruce/Dreamstime.com, 131bl Dreamstime.com, 132bl Kamil fazrin Rauf/Dreamstime.com, 133tl Yves Forestier/CORBIS SYGMA, 133cr Richard T. Nowitz/CORBIS, 135tl Doconnell/Dreamstime.com, 135tr Dreamstime.com, 135bl Loke Yek Mang/Dreamstime.com, 136-137 Asther Lau Choon Siew/Dreamstime.com, 137tl Alistair Scott/Dreamstime.com, 137bl Ilya Gridnev/Dreamstime.com, 138-139 Dreamstime.com, 139tl Lucian Coman/Dreamstime.com, 139bl Chris Townsend/Dreamstime.com, 140 Lorraine Swanson/Dreamstime.com, 141tr Roger Ressmeyer/CORBIS, 141bl all Dreamstime.com, 142 Ryszard Bednarek/Dreamstime.com, 143tr Alex Hinds/Dreamstime.com, 143br Owen Franken/Corbis, 144-145 Jeff Lewis/Icon SMI/Corbis, 145tr Eddie Saab/Dreamstime.com, 146cr Dean Hoch/Dreamstime.com, 146b Gabe Palmer/CORBIS, 147tc Visuals Unlimited/Corbis, 147br Fred Goldstein/Dreamstime.com, 148tl Peter Dazeley/zefa/Corbis, 148bl Roger Ressmeyer/CORBIS, 148-149 John W. Gertz/zefa/Corbis, 149br Reuters/CORBIS, 150-151 Visuals Unlimited/Corbis, 152-153 Dreamstime.com, 153tr Dreamstime.com, 154bc Gordana Sermek/Dreamstime.com, 155t Dreamstime.com, 155bl Vladimir Pomortsev/Dreamstime.com, 156bl Daniel Gustavsson/Dreamstime.com, 157br Franz Pfluegl/Dreamstime.com, 158-159 Visuals Unlimited/Corbis, 159br Milan Kopcok/Dreamstime.com, 161tc Dreamstime.com, 161br Yanik Chauvin/Dreamstime.com, 162bl Reuters/CORBIS, 163tl Brett Mulcahy/Dreamstime.com, 163br Sandy Matzen/Dreamstime.com, 164b Dreamstime.com, 165tr Darrell Young/Dreamstime.com, 165br Simone Van Den Berg/Dreamstime.com, 166bl Patrik Giardino/CORBIS, 167tr Natalie Fobes/CORBIS, 167br NASA, 168 Richard T. Nowitz/CORBIS, 169tl Dreamstime.com, 169br Louie Psihoyos/CORBIS, 170 Adrian Moisei/Dreamstime.com, 171tr Jack Schiffer/Dreamstime.com, 171br Darius Ramazani/zefa/Corbis